Harnessing Technology for Every Child Matters and Personalised Learning

Services for children are changing in many ways, not least schools: new ones are being built; more practitioners fulfil more diverse roles; the testing and assessment regime is changing; and new technologies enable us to teach pupils both well established and completely new curriculum areas in ways that are more engaging.

Underpinning these transformations are three core policies: 'Every Child Matters', 'Personalised Learning' and 'Harnessing Technology'. Combined, they are at the heart of changes to children's and young people's experiences of school. This book considers these policies and their interlinked relationship, making it an essential resource for training and practising teachers, school leaders and all those involved in educational transformation.

To achieve the five outcomes of the 'Every Child Matters' agenda requires an approach that is pupil-centred, with developments in new technologies making it possible not only to understand each individual more precisely, but also for pupils to learn in more flexible and personalised ways. Through innovations such as web-based information sharing, learning platforms and e-portfolios, schools will be able to offer content appropriate to pupils' personal goals, going beyond conventional orthodoxies of time and place.

How far these policies will transform schools and services for children and young people remains to be seen. Consideration is given to the barriers to their success, the issues that impinge on them, and questions asked about their capacity to bring about long-term, systemic change.

John Galloway is Advisory Teacher for ICT/SEN and Inclusion in Tower Hamlets. He also lectures, works as an educational consultant, and writes for national newspapers.

Harnessing Technology for Every Child Matters and Personalised Learning

John Galloway

Routledge
Taylor & Francis Group

LONDON AND NEW YORK

First published 2009
by Routledge
2 Park Square, Milton Park, Abingdon, Oxon OX14 4RN

Simultaneously published in the USA and Canada
by Routledge
270 Madison Avenue, New York, NY 10016

Routledge is an imprint of the Taylor & Francis Group, an informa business

© 2009 John Galloway

Typeset in Sabon by
Taylor & Francis Books
Printed and bound in Great Britain by
CPI Antony Rowe, Chippenham, Wiltshire

British Library Cataloguing in Publication Data
A catalogue record for this book is available from the British Library

Library of Congress Cataloging in Publication Data
Galloway, John R. (John Robert), 1958-
Harnessing technology for Every Child Matters and personalised learning /
John Galloway.
    p. cm.
Includes bibliographical references.
    1. Educational technology–Great Britain. 2. Education and state–Great
Britain. 3. Educational equalization–Great Britain. 4. Motivation in education–
Great Britain. I. Title.
    LB1028.3.G35 2008
    371.330941–dc22
                            2008021894

ISBN 13: 978-0-415-45871-9 (pbk)
ISBN 13: 978-0-203-42648-7 (ebk)

Contents

Acknowledgements

First of all I would like to thank my wife, Annie, for all those long, lonely evenings without which I would never have been able to write this book. And then my children, for whom it must have seemed at times that every child mattered – except them. I also need to thank the ever-generous spirit of the teaching profession, which always has so many good stories to tell of interesting ways of working, as exemplified by my colleagues in the smartest ICT Advisory Team in the country. Thanks are also due to those who helped me with content intended specifically for this book, particularly Theresa Knox of Ealing EOTAS service, and Stephen Byrne of Gumley House Convent School, Hounslow. Last, but not least, my thanks to Karen Pollard from the Cherokee project in Bath, and her student, "Lizzie", who gave me an insight into what it is like to be an e-learner through her well considered answers.

John Galloway
May 2008

Preface

Every Child Matters and ICT – A Day in the Life, 2010

Tiffany is late logging on for school. She should have accessed today's Creative Media work before 10 am, as was agreed in her Personal Education Plan, but by five past 10 there is no sign of her. A text message has been generated automatically by the system and sent to her foster carer, Darren Jenks, and copied to her form tutor Jeff Randle, who will follow it up later when she comes in for her Maths class. He wants to see her anyway.

When her timetable was first organised, at the planning meeting when Tiffany moved in with the Jenkses, the string of late marks on the records transferred electronically from her previous school was a concern. However, because the Ablair Academy is a full service school, with courses shared with the adult education section going right into the evening, and a well established online learning platform, a lot of flexibility was possible. Jeff Randle had analysed Tiffany's performance data, right through from her early learning milestones in the Foundation Stage to the records updated only yesterday, using RAISEonline. It soon became obvious that, apart from a dip earlier in the year, which coincided with the uncertainty around her placement, she was doing fine. The lateness really seemed to be because, as Tiffany said, 'I'm not a morning person.' So her timetable includes a mixture of classes, some in the early evenings, others at the local further education college for a vocational course in 'retail interfaces for mobile technologies', and even some online work accessed from home. She particularly likes these as she can sit on her bed and use her laptop, music playing, coffee to hand, and within easy shouting distance of either Darren or his wife Megan, should she have a problem.

Which is what happened this particular morning, when the logon failed. Darren traced the source of the problem to where he had disabled the wireless hub because the boy across the road had again hacked the password and was surfing at his expense. An email to Mr Randle reassured the school, and pretty soon Tiffany was getting on with fine-tuning the narrative for her computer game, the assessment deadline for which was getting close.

Despite the messages, Tiffany had been very much on Jeff Randle's mind that morning, as he was preparing to update her Common Assessment Framework. Although he isn't the Designated Teacher for Children in Public

Care in the school, it had been agreed that he would be the Lead Professional for her, so he has to coordinate all the other people involved and keep an oversight on what's happening. As the form is online, an e-CAF, Jeff, Lynne Webster, her social worker, and Jas Kaur, a psychotherapist from the Child and Adolescent Mental Health Team, are each going to review and update it before lunchtime.

Working together over the internet has been made easier by the local information-sharing agreement that allows different agencies to share and exchange data about children and young people to varying degrees. All three can open and add to Tiffany's particular records because they have been given specific access, something they won't automatically have for every child's files. Jeff normally wouldn't see detailed records for looked-after children – like most of his colleagues, he would simply see a flag on ContactPoint that showed other people were working with Tiffany, so he could contact them directly if he needed to.

Once the form is complete, it seems that generally Tiffany's placement with the Jenkses is going well, but she doesn't seem to be making friends, even after eight weeks. The timetable could be a problem, as she is in several different groups, with the exception of afternoon registration three days a week. Jeff thinks they could look outside school, so he texts Tiffany to ask her to meet him at 4:30 that afternoon, before her GCSE Maths class. As Megan Jenks has also signed up for the course, he suggests Tiffany invite her along too.

When they arrive, Jeff Randle has pulled up the online list of local groups that offer out-of-school activities. Tiffany likes the idea of having some fun away from school, and opts for an outdoor pursuits course that the authority has commissioned the local Scouts to provide. It has good feedback on the website and it is mixed, so there's the chance of meeting someone 'fit', as she put it.

That evening, Tiffany remembers to update her blog, as she hasn't done it for a while. She is part of a virtual community on a secure site especially for looked-after children, so she and her carers know it is quite safe to use. She wasn't sure what to put, so just said, 'No change.'

Not for Tiffany, perhaps, but technology is bringing about changes with reverberations that will bring shifts in the education system, making fundamental differences to children's experiences of schooling – and to the way they are supported generally. We will know them better, track their achievement more accurately and sensitively, be able to take into account preferences for content and delivery of education, and even educate them beyond the current school boundaries of time and place. This book is about those changes.

Introduction

In recent years, the Labour government has worked to change the way that services for children work, in a number of fundamental ways. What follows is an exploration of those strategies, an explanation of their interrelatedness, and a consideration of their practical impact.

Legislation has sought to change practice by bringing support services closer together to work in a more collaborative way, mainly under the Every Child Matters agenda. This was brought into law in the 2004 Education Act, which arose from the Laming Inquiry into the death of Victoria Climbié. Separation between Education Authorities and Social Care was removed, and Children's Services came into being to bring about more joined-up working, headed up by a Director of Children's Services – a post responsible for all the frontline services a local authority might provide.

While seeking to pursue a more holistic remit for support services, requiring all agencies to work together more closely (by creating Children's Trusts), public services have also been moving in a direction that aims to 'personalise' them. Instead of recipients being given whatever service is provided locally, the intention is to give them a degree of control over the process and the provision allocated.

In education, this has introduced a notion of Personalised Learning. Here the intention to put the individual's needs at the centre of service delivery is manifested in a belief that pupils' educational experiences should be based on the most effective way for them to learn, and to some degree what interests them, rather than the very prescriptive methodologies and content that existed previously, and largely still exist, in schools. Since its introduction as a policy goal in 2004, this concept has begun to shift from a somewhat nebulous idea to something more concrete, defined through *2020 Vision* (DfES, 2006), a report headed by the incoming Chief Inspector of Schools at that time (and therefore Head of Ofsted), Christine Gilbert. This clarified that the process of learning, rather than the content, was the main target of personalisation. That is, skills and capabilities should be the focus of education, rather than the knowledge and facts that were imparted. This is not to say that there is no role for subjects, but that there is a need for a shift in the delivery of education to focusing on how something is learned, as well as what has been taken in, remembered and understood. There is also a need to recognise the shifting nature of knowledge, driven by new technologies – that through the web we can find whatever we need to know, whenever we need to know it – just-in-time learning, rather than just-in-case. We need the skills to find information, assess its validity, reflect on it, and repurpose it for whatever task we are engaged in.

Alongside these changes in the model of provision of services to children came developments in information and communication technologies (ICT) that could make the changes viable, and act as a spur to add impetus to them. ICT is central both to supporting these changes and to galvanising them, acting as an integral element, but also as a catalyst, enabling activities that previously were not possible. The ambitions for the role of such technologies are outlined in *Harnessing Technology* (DfES, 2005a), the government's e-strategy – sub-titled *Transforming Learning and Children's Services*. While looking to provide the necessary conditions for ICT to be central to pupils' educational experiences, and therefore to play a significant role in personalisation, it also aims to deliver a framework that will support them more holistically through information-sharing, early identification and intervention when there are difficulties, and involving parents more closely.

This book explores the implementation of these policies and the central role of ICT in their delivery. It deals with the separate requirements of each, and also the overlap and interaction that can bring about fundamental changes to the English education system and, more broadly, services to children. It is illustrated throughout with case studies, practical examples and interviews, to put some realistic meat on the theoretical skeleton, to show how policy is becoming practice and the education and children's services environments are changing. Examples are also given of resources, mainly websites and software titles, that are being used to help bring these changes into place. The inclusion of these titles does not necessarily mean endorsement of them, and as with many things in the fast-moving world of new technologies, there can be no guarantee of their continued existence.

To begin, there is a brief overview of how each agenda came about and how they fit together. All are works in progress that have been reviewed and developed since their first inception. Chapter One looks at what has been achieved so far, with examples of activities that show what the policies look like in practice and how they support each other in implementation.

Chapter Two goes on to discuss why and how technology has made a difference, the ways of working it has enabled, and the possibilities for the future. It discusses how the advances in technology have brought changes in practice that were previously not possible, and how these changes will continue in the near future.

In Chapter Three there is a sharper focus on how ICT provides a web of support for children through holding and sharing information, and its use in identifying when and how children need support. This extends from professionals collaborating on jointly held case notes to teachers reviewing educational progress over time. These approaches also provide a way of reaching out to those on, and even beyond, the fringes of education and the reach of support services, offering new ways to include the socially disadvantaged and excluded.

The possibilities for multiple ways of working also extend to learning. Chapter Four looks at how technology breaks the traditional boundaries of learning at particular times and in particular places, and how, as a result, learning can be personalised rather than homogenised. As Dan Buckley says of the curriculum shift he proposes in *The Personalisation by Pieces Framework*:

> In developing a curriculum fit for the 21st Century we are recognising the central importance of new technologies working together with our growing understanding of how learning works. Throughout this framework we are assuming that children in the near future will each have a learning device at least as powerful as current laptops. If this is the case then the small scale model set up in schools with the purpose of growing capacity for personalisation must be technology rich.
>
> (Buckley, 2007: 29)

Not only can the curriculum be provided in different formats and at different times and places, but also ICT can track progress and provide guidance and appropriate content. Many of these changes are happening already through the collaborative, creative and communicative tools offered on the internet. However, schools have only just begun to exploit the possibilities offered by these advances, and the limited access many pupils suffer may exacerbate the iniquity of the digital divide.

Finally, there is a consideration of the disjunct between the policy objectives and the practical possibilities – whether these objectives are realistic, or whether they will be modified in their application by the existing systemic demands of both entrenched processes and experienced practitioners.

Chapter 1

Policy development and interconnection

Each of the various strategies and policies developed in recent years to meet the needs of and to support children and young people has an individual identity and purpose; they are also closely interlinked, and to some degree the success and development of each is dependent on the others. Here the policies are briefly outlined and the interdependence drawn out – starting with the role of ICT, as in some senses it has a service function for the other strategies to build on. They cannot be fully implemented without it, and they also give purpose to the faith and money invested in it.

Harnessing technology

In 2004, the Department for Education and Skills (subsequently the Department for Children, Schools and Families) launched *Harnessing Technology, Transforming Learning and Children's Services*, a five-year strategy for change – although it had shown its faith in ICT before that. Since its election in 1997, this government has demonstrated its belief in the transformational abilities of ICT through its heavy investment in resources, infrastructure and training. While there is much debate about the efficacy of this expenditure – involving both those who think it has been wasted and those who think it is too little – it can be seen as part of a long-term strategy.

Spending in education began by concentrating on increasing the number of machines in schools, then moved on to connecting them all up and ensuring staff knew how to use them. This saw funds ring-fenced to be spent on hardware and on fast connections, and dedicated funds for training to bring all teachers up to a national standard, with an ICT skills requirement added to the prerequisites for achieving Qualified Teacher Status alongside Maths and English.

Annual surveys have monitored these changes, showing for instance that in 1998, the average primary school had one computer for every 18 pupils. By 2007 that had become 6.2 pupils per computer. A similar shift has happened in secondary schools, from 9.1 pupils to each computer to 3.6. Although these might be considered crude measures, as the quantity of machines does not determine the quality of learning they are used for, it does show the growth of penetration of ICT in state schools. The discussion is also made more complex by the range of devices that are now used in teaching and learning, no longer just desktop and laptop computers, but handhelds, tablets and even mobile phones.

The measures for connectivity have become less important. It is taken for granted now that all schools are connected to the internet with fast broadband access, compared with only 17 per cent of primaries in 1997. With the growth of mobile connectivity through wireless and phones, and home broadband access rates of more than 60 per cent, the expectation of being connected not only at school, but at any time or place is developing. Regional broadband consortia have been established to create a National Learning Network, with schools and libraries connected across authorities, and authorities across regions. In London, for instance, the London Grid for Learning was established, one of ten such consortia. Not since the demise of the Inner London Education Authority in 1990 had there been such a collaborative endeavour across the capital, only this time involving more boroughs, all 32 of them. This cooperation saw institutions able to negotiate preferential rates for procurement of the infrastructure to connect up state schools across the region, along with the learning portal running on it, and subsequently content and software for use in class. This includes, for instance, a deal whereby clips from the British Pathe News film library can be downloaded free by teachers while working on a computer connected to the Grid.

Alongside the provision of hardware and a network infrastructure, there was also a need for staff to be skilled in using what had now become available. A large-scale training programme funded from the National Lottery's New Opportunities Fund was instigated (hence it was known as NoF training). This spent £230 million[1] on bringing practising teachers' skills up to scratch – but had only limited success. One of the reasons for this was the mode of delivery: much of it had to be undertaken in teachers' own time, often using distance training materials, with no means of ensuring engagement. (In contrast to the Numeracy and Literacy Strategies, through which all primary teachers had five full days' training in each.)

From 1999, all newly qualified teachers have had to achieve a mandatory level of skills in order to qualify. This is now administered by an online test of competence. Those successfully completing it are given a certificate to show they have met this requirement.

There has also been considerable investment in content for teachers to use on the machines provided. Not only have regional broadband consortia been expected to negotiate aggregated rates for online resources, but schools have received 'e-learning credits' to spend specifically on software. This was ring-fenced money that could be spent only on programs that had met a set of criteria sufficient for them to be approved for inclusion on a designated website.

This was partly in response to an investment of £75 million provided for the BBC to develop online curriculum materials (known as BBC Jam – see Chapter

Two for examples of the content). To assuage concerns about a lack of competition in the delegation of this money, very stringent conditions were placed on it, determining the breadth of curriculum coverage, the need for commissioning from third parties, and that all mainstream resources had to be produced in four languages – English, Welsh, Scots Gaelic and Irish – in order to be accessible to all pupils in the member countries of the United Kingdom.

This investment saw the development of some truly innovative and original materials. However, despite the stringent conditions imposed, BBC Jam was challenged by software development companies and fell foul of EU competition regulations. Having been withdrawn from public use in 2006, it was eventually announced in March 2007 that the BBC Governors had decided to pull the plug on it, despite the considerable investment of public funds.

Moving forward with ICT

The government had put into place resources (both hardware and software), an extensive and all-inclusive network for schools, and a workforce that was becoming increasingly confident in using these tools (81 per cent of secondary teachers expressed confidence in their abilities to teach with ICT in 2004; Prior and Hall, 2003). But this is not the whole story.

There is a cautionary note from Ofsted (2005b) in its report *Embedding ICT in Schools*, in which it observes that while staff competence and confidence have improved, this is more in using the applications themselves than in using them effectively in learning and teaching. There remains a tendency to stick to safe, tried-and-tested approaches to classroom practice. More optimistically, there is evidence that this increased confidence has led some teachers to try new approaches and activities, and to discover for themselves the impact on pupils and on the teaching and learning process (Condie *et al.*, 2007: 19).

As the impact of resourcing schools and training staff began to take effect, the new strategy began to move towards 'e-maturity'. Although this was not the end of initiatives to tackle specific aspects of ICT in education, it marked an overall shift to a more strategic view. In 2007, for instance, attention turned to the digital divide: the perceived gap between those who have easy access to ICT (usually at home) and the learning benefits this brings, and those who do not – often considered to be determined by income and social class. (However, this is a more complex issue than at first glance: pupils from low-income families may have computers and connectivity, but they might not be using them for learning.)

To address this, the Computers for Pupils scheme was launched. This is designed to provide secondary-age pupils from the most deprived wards across the country with a computer to use at home and a connection to the internet. Funding was provided to local authorities using a formula that took into account the index of multiple deprivation and free school meals, then, as 50 per cent of these pupils were thought likely to have access already, divided the total by two.

However, there was clearly a belief that ICT was becoming embedded and needed less targeted expenditure, as previously ring-fenced monies now became part of a more generic Harnessing Technology grant, allocated through local authorities.

The Harnessing Technology strategy itself also began to shift at this point. At its launch, it had four main foci:

- transform teaching, learning and help to improve outcomes for children, young people, and adults through shared ideas, more exciting lessons and online help for professionals
- engage 'hard-to-reach' learners with special needs support, more motivating ways of learning, and more choice about how and where to learn
- build an open, accessible system, with more information and services online for parents and carers, children, young people, adult learners and employers; and more cross-organisation collaboration to improve personalised support and choice
- achieve greater efficiency and effectiveness, with online research, access to shared ideas and lessons plans, improved systems and processes in children's services, shared procurement and easier administration.

(DfES, 2005a)

By the 2007 review of the strategy, these had been crystallised to become:

- fit-for-purpose technology, systems and resources
- capability and capacity of the workforce, providers and learners
- efficiency, effectiveness and value for money across the system
- improving learner and system performance.

(Becta, 2007c)

The responsibility for delivery had also shifted from the department itself to its technology agency, Becta,[2] a quango that started life as the National Council for Educational Technology. These crisper, updated aims suggest the strategy has a clearer direction, as expected as it matures and as changes occur throughout the education system. There is more concern with systemic issues than with the experiences and needs of learners, suggesting that pedagogy and process have been addressed, and it is the ability of the system to provide support for these that now needs sorting out. However, this is not quite the case, as each of the updated aims has sub-aims. These, for example, talk about leaders having 'knowledge and skills'; learners having 'greater choice in learning opportunities' and 'access to appropriate technology'; and practitioners collaborating to 'share good practice and learning resources'.

There is a clearer understanding of the tasks necessary to give ICT its central role in transforming education and children's services, not least because we are beginning to see practical examples and are gaining an appreciation of what the policy means in practice, as highlighted in this and subsequent chapters.

Every Child Matters

The Every Child Matters strategy was released in 2003, shortly before the e-strategy. Its agenda of changing the landscape of services, both universal and specialised for children and young people, is reflected in the latter's extended title, *Harnessing Technology: Transforming Learning and Children's Services*. While Harnessing Technology is informed by Every Child Matters, the changes had yet to be introduced through the Children Act 2004 so at this point they were aspirational rather than actual, but they did help prepare the ground for the reforms to come.

These changes included the unifying of education and children's social care services into Children's Services through the merger of Local Education Authorities with Children's Social Services. Similarly, the posts of Director of Education and Director of Children's Social Services merged to become Director of Children's Services (although this amalgamation was not made mandatory). The Local Education Authority became simply the Local Authority. While Health Services remain outside the framework, there is an expectation of close working relationships to provide a regime of holistic support, both universal and specialised.

These joint working relationships will become more formalised through the creation of Children's Trusts. While there is no statutory requirement for Local Authorities to establish these, there is an expectation that all will do so. They are partnerships of services for children in a particular area and, alongside Health and Children's Services, will include the voluntary sector and extended schools (DfES, 2005b).

This latter is one practical application of thinking about children's needs more broadly and working cooperatively to meet them. The extended schools programme was established in 2002 in response to the needs of pupils and families in deprived areas. By providing additional curriculum activities, support for parents and access to other services, they are intended to raise standards by recognising and addressing the fact that no matter how good a teacher is, there are times when other areas of difficulty in pupils' lives impinge on their educational performance.

In 2005, the government declared that all schools should become extended schools as part of the joined-up working of Children's Trusts, although without determining specifically what one is. The intention is that they will have:

- high-quality 'wraparound' childcare provided on the school site or through other local providers, with supervised transfer arrangements where appropriate, available 8 am–6 pm all year round

- a varied menu of activities on offer, such as homework clubs and study support, sport (at least two hours a week beyond the school day for those who want it), music tuition, dance and drama, arts and crafts, special interest clubs such as chess and first-aid courses, visits to museums and galleries, learning a foreign language, volunteering, business and enterprise activities
- parenting support, including information sessions for parents at key transition points, parenting programmes run with the support of other children's services and family learning sessions to allow children to learn with their parents
- swift and easy referral to a wide range of specialist support services such as speech therapy, child and adolescent mental health services, family support services, intensive behaviour support, and (for young people) sexual health services (some may be delivered on school sites)
- providing wider community access to ICT, sports and arts facilities, including adult learning.

(DfES, 2005b)

However, not every activity or provision has to be on site; they can be organised collaboratively; and some aspects of them (such as hours of childcare above a certain threshold) may attract a fee. Not all services will be co-located, that is, based at the school; however this will be the case to some degree at one school in each local authority, enabling easier multi-agency support.

There are also changes in the way support agencies are expected to work together. In the first instance, referrals between agencies will be standardised around a Common Assessment Framework (CAF), except in circumstances where a statutory system exists, such as in child protection cases where a prescribed threshold for support has been passed. The CAF is based on a previous Department of Health assessment process focusing on three elements – child, family and environment.

No matter which service, nor which practitioner within it, starts the process of looking for further support for a child or young person, there is an expectation that this assessment procedure will be followed, in order to determine what action to take and what other agencies need to become involved. One element of the thinking behind this is that previously families have had to retell their stories several times, in different ways, to each professional they have encountered as more have become involved, or as each fresh intervention has started. Another aim is to give the family, and the child, greater control within the referral process. This extends to determining how information can be shared, and with whom. Parents are asked to sign that they understand the purposes for which the information has been given, or in some cases, under 'Gillick competence',[3] children themselves can sign and also specify who it can be shared with, or from whom it should be withheld. (In some instances, where a child is in immediate danger of harm, for instance, this need for consent may be overridden; however in such an instance the referral has passed a statutory threshold so the CAF is no longer the applicable referral.)

It is increasingly common for local authorities to require all services to make their paperwork 'CAF-compliant', that is, using common form fields and information requirements, so that if ever a referral needs to be made, a large part of the work has already been done. However, even if most of the information has already been compiled and can be gathered together easily, the expectation is still that the child and their parents have a role in completing it, and the requirements for consent will remain unchanged.

While the CAF is already established (by Summer 2007) across England, there is an expectation that an electronic version will be in place before 2010. This should make collection and sharing of information, and its secure storage and transfer, easier.

Sharing information is one of the key aspects of Every Child Matters, and was given a statutory basis in the Children Act. One provision is for a database of all children from birth until the age of 18 to be established and made available nationally by early 2009. Known as ContactPoint, it will contain limited, key information:

- name, address, gender, date of birth, and an identifying number of all children in England (up to their 18th birthday)
- name and contact details for:
  - parents or carers
  - educational setting (e.g. school name)
  - primary medical practitioner (e.g. GP practice)
- other services.

(DCSF, 2007b)

The inclusion of all children between these ages aims to ensure universal entitlement to core services, and recognises the fact that it is not possible to predict precisely who will need support during their young lives (although another key theme is early identification and intervention). For those children and young people for whom an intervention is already in place, a flag may be attached to their record indicating that someone is working with them. Such an attachment will also be made to show that an assessment – although not specifically what sort – has been undertaken. Some practitioners may also add a third type of flag to show that they have additional information related to the child that may be of relevance to other agencies, although again the nature of the information will not be shown, and if contacted, whether the information should be shared will be up to the professional judgement of whoever attached the flag. In some instances, additional information, for example concerning substance abuse or sexual health, will need consent to be included.

There is, understandably, considerable concern about the number of people who will be able to see potentially sensitive information about young people who may be very vulnerable – and the ease of access to it. This is why access to these records will be not be available to all professionals, but limited to users who are authorised and trained. Alongside this, there will be stringent security requirements with users having to have both a password and a PIN number, and a physical security token, probably a USB key or smart card, which they will need to use in order to complete their log-on to ContactPoint.

While this kind of generic information may be held by several agencies, and so is in some senses already available, the novelty is in bringing it together and providing speedy, although limited, access to it. The intention is to create a system whereby practitioners can easily share information and concerns, to identify difficulties earlier, and to make collaborative working easier.

As well as information-sharing, there is expected to be closer cooperation between agencies working together. Where more than one agency is involved, a lead professional will head up the 'team around the child', coordinating the work and acting as the main point of contact with the family. Here, too, ICT plays a role, allowing for the compilation of multi-agency case notes. One development of the CAF is the 'e-CAF', an online version that makes it easier for professionals both to contribute their information, and in some versions, to develop a joint chronology once the child has been referred to them. In this way it is expected that each person involved will see what work others are doing, and how they are each contributing to the collective approach (see Chapter 3).

Personalised learning

The intention of Every Child Matters is to put the focus clearly on children and their needs. They are the central focus of any work, and the support systems and working practices of the professionals are expected to shift to reflect this. This is also the intention of Personalised Learning, the education policy that represents a philosophical shift in the provision of state-run services generally. The belief is that systems need to work for the benefit of users rather than for their own ends, as demonstrated by the introduction of choice in the National Health Service, with patients being able to select the consultant they want to see and have some say in the date and time of their appointments.

Since this approach to learning in schools was announced in January 2004, by (then) Education Secretary David Miliband, 'Personalised Learning' has been a much-used term – and also a frequently abused one. It has its origins in a political agenda that promotes equality of opportunity – the belief that everyone, regardless of background or circumstances, has a right to achieve to the best of their abilities, and to have high aspirations that state-provided services will support and promote.

Miliband gave an early definition:

> This is what I mean by 'Personalised Learning'. High expectations of every child, given practical form by high quality teaching based on a

sound knowledge and understanding of each child's needs. It is not individualised learning where pupils sit alone at a computer. Nor is it pupils left to their own devices – which too often reinforces low aspirations. It can only be developed school by school. It cannot be imposed from above.

(Speech to North of England Education Conference, January 2004)

This does not sound like a revolutionary approach to education. One would hope that all teachers and schools already aim for 'high-quality teaching' and a high level of 'understanding of each child's needs', and that they always have. The innovative aspect of this agenda becomes evident in the elements outlined as being necessary to achieve it:

- Assessment for Learning that feeds into lesson planning and teaching strategies, sets clear targets, and clearly identifies what pupils need to do to get there
- a wide range of teaching techniques to promote a broad range of learning strategies, facilitated by high quality ICT that promotes individual and group learning as well as teaching
- curriculum choice, particularly from the age of 14, and the development of subject specialism
- the organisation of the school, including the structure of the day and of lessons, using workforce reform to enhance teaching and learning and to ensure consistency
- links to services beyond the classroom, involving the wider community and families, parents, providing strong support; and the engagement of LEAs in the agenda set out in the *Every Child Matters* Green Paper.

(*Ibid.*)

In order to clarify further what Personalised Learning might mean in practice, a number of activities took place following its inception. First, a 'National Conversation about Personalised Learning' to try to engage the teaching profession and other interested parties in identifying what was already happening, where it was already in evidence. Subsequent to this, a report was commissioned from a review group chaired by Christine Gilbert (who subsequently became Her Majesty's Chief Inspector, Ofsted), at the beginning of 2006, by (then) Education Secretary Ruth Kelly. The remit was to 'present to the Secretary of State a vision for personalised teaching and learning in 2020 which enables every child to achieve higher standards; and to make recommendations which would support delivery of that vision.'

This they duly did (DfES, 2006), giving an outline based around two criteria: 'learner-centred and knowledge-centred', and 'assessment-centred'. The first of these is outlined as:

Close attention is paid to learners' knowledge, skills, understanding and attitudes. Learning is connected to what they already know (including from outside the classroom). Teaching enthuses pupils and engages their interest in learning: it identifies, explores and corrects misconceptions. Learners are active and curious: they create their own hypotheses, ask their own questions, coach one another, set goals for themselves, monitor their progress and experiment with ideas for taking risks, knowing that mistakes and 'being stuck' are part of learning. Work is sufficiently varied and challenging to maintain their engagement but not so difficult as to discourage them. This engagement allows learners of all abilities to succeed, and it avoids the disaffection and attention-seeking that give rise to problems with behaviour.

(*Ibid.*: 6)

While many might comment that much of what is listed here is simply good practice, there is a theme of pupils' responsibility for their own learning, and for supporting each other, that marks it out. Similarly, with the encouragement of risk-taking and seeing mistakes as learning opportunities, rather than an emphasis on target-driven, results-oriented success, there is a shift in focus.

The second element of the review's definition similarly puts the pupil at the centre of the process. Although teachers are clearly instrumental in driving the assessment process, the purpose is to inform pupils and help them to understand and to make decisions about their learning. Assessment is both formative and summative, and supports learning: learners monitor their progress and, with their teachers, identify their next steps. Techniques such as open questioning, sharing learning objectives and success criteria, and focused marking have a powerful effect on the extent to which learners are enabled to take an active role in their learning. Sufficient time is always given for learners' reflection.

Whether individually or in pairs, they review what they have learnt and how they have learnt it. Their evaluations contribute to their understanding. They know their levels of achievement and make progress towards their goals.

(*Ibid.*)

Despite the intentions of Personalised Learning and its five key elements being outlined from the very beginning of the policy, and then its clarification by the incoming Chief Inspector of Schools, it remains open to reinterpretation by schools.

This was one of the findings of the review *Impact 2007: Personalising Learning with Technology* (Underwood *et al.*, 2007), which defines the concept as 'the tailoring of pedagogy, curriculum and learning support to meet the needs and aspirations of individual learners, irrespective of ability, culture or social status, in order to nurture the unique talents of every pupil'. Despite this quite pragmatic understanding, the review found that 'There is discontinuity between managers, staff and pupils as to what personalising learning actually means in practice; this discontinuity also applies to policy makers.' (*Ibid.*: para. 6.3)

This may be a reflection of its mixed heritage, an educational concept with political roots – one that has semantic similarities to previous theoretical underpinnings of educational processes, such as 'child-centred education' and 'individualised learning'. However, the many interpretations are spawning a similar number of implementations, seeded by government grants to all schools (in excess of £300 million for Key Stage 3 in 2007–08), many of which involve ICT, and some of which seem genuinely to be trying to put the true spirit of the government's intent into practice.

Policies in practice – working together

All three of these major policy initiatives have at their heart the intention to benefit each individual child by bringing them more clearly into focus so that services can be tailored to meet their unique needs. By knowing them better, and monitoring their progress and development, we should be able to support them more effectively to help them become fulfilled human beings. Some of this is becoming easier through the application of technology, and some is only just becoming possible.

We can know children more clearly through gathering, analysing and sharing information. While this is not new, ICT offers novel ways of delivering assessments, as well as new forms of assessment. There can also be a greater degree of analysis, both deeper and more sophisticated. This leads to a capacity to channel tasks refined by this information to pupils. For some time now, schools have been using centrally provided tools to monitor pupils' performance over time, tracking their progress in the end-of-key-stage SATs assessments. First there was the Pupil Achievement Tracker (PAT), and Performance and Analysis (PANDA), which monitored individual and institutional performance, respectively. Both have now been replaced by the more sophisticated RAISEonline (Reporting and Analysis for Improvement through School Self-Evaluation, www.raiseonline.org), which performs both functions. With this system, it is possible to interrogate the data from large data sets (such as whole school, year group, class, gender, ethnicity and so on) to individual pupils, down to the level of a particular question in a given test. Although the data are managed centrally, schools have the capacity to download the tools and add their own to give greater depth. Ofsted uses RAISEonline for its judgements, so many schools add further information to contextualise and provide better understanding of what the figures mean (see Chapter Two).

The kinds of information schools might upload includes Cognitive Abilities Tests (CATs).[4] These short tests measure verbal, non-verbal and numerical reasoning, and are considered an accurate predictor of GCSE results (which is preferred in some secondary schools to SATs as indicators of pupil ability on first entry). Increasingly, tests of this type are computerised, with computer-generated reports, often with suggested programmes of study, and the technology even setting and marking work and monitoring progress (see Chapter Two for examples).

This is one promoted benefit of the provision of a learning platform (see Chapter 3), an online educational resource that brings together suitable content, with tools for working, and means of collaborating with peers and communicating with teachers for feedback and assessment. This is an integral element of the Building Schools for the Future programme, a long-term strategy to rebuild or refurbish every secondary school in the country. Part of the provision being made under this scheme is for ICT – 10 per cent of the expenditure – with learning platforms being a specific element of this.

There is, understandably, some scepticism about the degree to which education can be reduced to an automated, machine-driven process, but there are as yet no solid examples of computers being able to reach any degree of sophistication beyond 'drill-and-practice' type programs, where learning takes place through repetition and memorising of content. However, such smooth integration of setting tasks, assessment, feedback and monitoring of progress is one of the intentions of the learning platform, sometimes referred to as either a virtual learning environment or a managed learning environment. The difference between these is that the former allows for the setting and receiving of work, whereas the latter is linked to the school's management information system, so can also feed data into reporting and monitoring.

Beyond recording and tracking school achievement, online databases also have other roles. They are being promoted to identify, monitor and keep track of children who may be considered vulnerable in some way. One such use is to support the work of Missing Children departments within Children's Services – another recent initiative whereby every authority is required to follow particular procedures to try to keep track of pupils who leave their area, or arrive in it, in order to reduce the number who disappear from the school system.

In addition, there are programs designed to identify children who are 'at risk' in some sense (although most of these have only been piloted, not implemented). Originally funded and monitored by the Office of the Deputy Prime Minister, a number of initiatives have been introduced. One example is RYOGENS (Reducing Youth Offending Generic Electronic National Solution), which allows practitioners to indicate concerns, chosen from around 40 criteria, that children are at risk of being drawn into offending behaviour. These indicators are weighted and, once a trigger point is reached, the system administrator is notified. As many of the indicators were considered to be not uniquely crime-related, the database was also seen as a means of highlighting children who were vulnerable in a more general sense. As any practitioner in an authority could access it and flag concerns, it was thought that this would act as a means to collate information about children – that while each professional might hold one small piece of information, when these were aggregated a more major issue might become clear.

While the structure for assessment of young people's needs is based on the three elements of development, family and environment, the desirable outcomes are usually couched in terms of the five threads of Every Child Matters. This approach is both holistic and future-facing, focusing on what are desirable outcomes for children and how they might be achieved. The five outcomes are:

- be healthy
- stay safe
- enjoy and achieve
- make a positive contribution
- achieve economic well-being.

This approach extends beyond considering the needs of individual children. To help those responsible for its delivery, at whatever level (school, local, regional or national), an Outcomes Framework was developed outlining the areas to be targeted under each heading and the criteria according to which these would be inspected.

In 'be healthy', for instance, health is taken to include physical, mental and sexual health, as well as knowing how to live a healthy lifestyle. Clearly ICT has a role in recording and monitoring the health of each individual, both for record-keeping and as part of curriculum activities, providing accurate, pertinent information at the time and place that it is needed.

Other ways it might help could be through the provision of self-help, counselling-style tools such as Ways Forward,[5] which provides a structure for users to think through the problems with which they are confronted. It has proved an effective way to engage in counselling young people who otherwise might not have done so, and has also given those who are untrained a way of structuring a conversation with someone who needs help to think through a situation.

'Stay safe' requires providers not only to ensure physical safety wherever children are – at school, or on a visit perhaps – but also to be free from abuse and violence. As well as the possibilities for assessing and monitoring mentioned above, ICT can also support proactive approaches such as providing a means of reporting bullying, or a forum for young people to share problems and experiences. One example of the former is Text Someone,[6] a very straightforward system that provides a secure, anonymous method for pupils to send a text message to alert their teachers to bullying, either of themselves or a friend, or of antisocial behaviour that they are aware of.

Learning, both formal and informal, is largely covered by 'enjoy and achieve'. While the role of ICT is well established in classrooms, it can also help pupils who are on the fringes of the system, such as those who are excluded, long-term sick or pregnant, by providing lessons for them wherever they are through online learning. As well as the facility many schools have through their own websites and portals, a number of companies, such as Accipio Learning,[7] have been supporting pupils outside school for some time.

Another way in which ICT can help pupils at school is in supporting good attendance. Truancy Call,[8] for instance, is a system that automatically links to a school's registration system and sends out a text message to parents when a child is marked as absent but no notification has been received from home. While contacting parents when pupils fail to arrive has been common practice for many years, by making the system automatic the alert can be generated much more quickly, and staff who are responsible for monitoring and supporting attendance can focus on more difficult cases.

In 'make a positive contribution' there is a requirement both to be law-abiding and not to become involved in antisocial behaviour, and also to promote participation in decision-making. Technology can help identify and monitor those considered to be at risk of misbehaving, or even offending; it also offers a range of ways in which pupils can become more proactive and involved in decisions concerning the matters that affect them in school. Views can be canvassed in a number of ways, such as using handheld voting devices in class or assembly, so that even those who may be reluctant to express an opinion have an opportunity to have theirs recorded; online forums, one of the resources expected to be included in a learning platform; or blogging around an issue, where a number of people reflect on a topic of mutual concern.

Despite the development of these tools, there remains a question as to whether pupils will be listened to, particularly in matters that affect them deeply but are considered beyond their capability to judge, such as teacher performance. Very rarely do schools involve pupils in providing feedback to staff on their teaching abilities. The web may become a means by which feedback is given – through posts on social networking sites, or unflattering videos on YouTube, or more formal platforms like the website RateMyTeachers.[9] This site allows pupils, or their parents, to record a mark out of five for any teacher in their school, for 'easiness' of the lessons, 'helpfulness' and 'clarity'. While this is clearly a site that could be used for the purpose of unwarranted and spiteful attacks on a teacher, it is also an opportunity that pupils are unlikely to get in any other way. As ways of working in schools shift, so will relationships between staff and pupils, hopefully making the use of such sites redundant. When pupils are able to take more responsibility for their learning, teacher effectiveness will come under closer scrutiny, requiring more openness about what is happening in classrooms.

The growth of e-commerce through the internet suggests that there should be myriad ways in which ICT can support the goal of helping all young people 'achieve economic well-being'. However, this relatively new possibility may not be something schools feel ready to offer, despite the National Curriculum including 'enterprise' as one of its cross-curricular themes. There is a recognition, though, of the role ICT skills have in employment, reflected in the forthcoming introduction of an ICT 'functional skills' element to GCSEs to provide a minimum standard for the award of qualifications.

E-portfolios, an electronic means of storing and disseminating work, will also enable pupils to show off what they have achieved, both in school and beyond, restructuring it for different audiences.

Beyond preparation for employment, schools can also help pupils prepare for later life by looking at managing their finances through the use of budgeting tools, and understanding aspects such as taxation and mortgages. This can be facilitated by using modelling tools, for instance a spreadsheet can be set up to demonstrate loan repayments at different rates over a range of time periods.

Conclusion

From the perspective of promoting the best interests of each and every child, personalising learning fits comfortably with the five outcomes outlined by Every Child Matters. And ICT can be seen to have a major role to play in bringing these about. There is a compatibility between the policies, although their practical implementation is only just beginning to demonstrate the transformation the policy-makers desire.

Chapter 2

What can the technology do for us?

Introduction

New technologies have not only made it possible to become more efficient at the things we have always done, but have also opened up new ways of working. Not just in working directly with children and young people, mainly in schools, but also for the professionals and practitioners around them, linking together to create networks of support. This chapter gives an overview of the array of devices and resources now available, and some accounts of how they are changing the education and children services landscape, and of how they are being used both to make every child matter and to personalise their learning.

What are ICTs?

The term ICT has slipped comfortably into everyday usage, at least in education. In other fields the middle C often remains absent. A fine distinction is sometimes used to distinguish between IT and ICT: IT is the tools – the equipment, infrastructure and resources, while ICT is the functions – what you can do with it. There are also times when the term becomes pluralised, 'information and communications technologies', reflecting the breadth of the subject and the range of resources it covers. No matter what term we use, it now covers a broad and expanding multitude of machines, capabilities and opportunities.

We no longer think of ICT as simply desktop computers. Developments in these technologies have produced both a range of new devices and the convergence of existing ones. As the technology has developed, so have our ways of using it. It is no longer predominantly about functions that streamline and automate office operations, as with word-processing and desktop publishing. More recent developments are about communicating, both receiving information from every niche across the planet, and also giving it out, connecting with millions of others, announcing ourselves and linking up with like-minded people.

Desktops are giving way to laptops, which come in many sizes and are becoming ever smaller. Keyboards are only one means of input; touch-sensitive surfaces have seen the birth of the tablet PC, and speech input is now included as standard, at least on computers with Windows operating systems. No longer is speaking to your computer an expensive add-on.

The personal digital assistant (PDA), an electronic diary and address book, is still with us, but tends to be grouped in the category of handhelds, devices that have just that quality. This can include phones, GPS navigators, music players, voice recorders, cameras – both still and video – and web browsers and email handlers, both alone and in almost any combination. Many also provide the typical office applications that first came with personal computers (PCs).

But they don't have to. Recent web developments have meant that devices can become more portable, and more flexible in use, by not being loaded with all the programs you could need. Instead, you access these as and when you need them through your internet connections. This can happen in two ways. One is to use online applications, such as Google Docs,[1] which runs on the internet but has the functionality you expect from a standard suite of office applications.

Another, not unrelated development is the use of 'thin client' technology, whereby the computer is considered to be a 'dumb terminal' with no useful programs installed and no files saved on it. Instead, both working documents and software are accessed through the internet, being hosted on a remote machine in a server-farm anywhere in the world.

These ways of working remove dependency on a personal computer. It becomes possible to access the files you want, with the software you need from any computer, anywhere – and even from any device. Applications such as Red Halo[2] are designed to work online to constantly monitor personal files and folders, regardless of the technology you are working on, and to update them automatically. So that next time you want to use a file, you can find it easily, in the latest version, and open, edit and save it on any device you happen to be using – whether a desktop machine in the office, or a games console on the train.

Our personal technologies are converging, and moving between them is becoming seamless. The photo you take with the camera on your mobile phone can be shared with the world and viewed on any convenient device within moments. Often this will be through the web or via phone function-ality; but wireless networks, Bluetooth and infrared also provide connections.

Once files have been shared, others can respond. The most recent incarna-tion of the internet (often referred to as Web 2.0) centres on this ability to connect and share, particularly around creative endeavours. A variety of tools have grown up that feed this development, such as YouTube[3] (used for sharing videos), Flickr[4] (an open-access photo album where users can upload in public and private areas), and Blogger[5] (space for online diaries or web-logs). These encourage interaction by allowing feedback to creators from those who have accessed their materials. Often such connectivity is used for chatting between friends, with messaging tools such as MSN, or through websites such as Facebook, which offer the opportunity to post personal information and connect with others. Beyond this is the possibility of working collaboratively and creatively with people you might only ever meet in a virtual world, sharing and contributing resources through one connected, online space, as with Second Life.

This kind of collaborative endeavour is already in use in both education and entertainment. Universities have for some years offered degree courses that are entirely online, using platforms such as First Class, Blackboard[6] and Moodle.[7] Typically students will be presented with artefacts, which could be text or other media, then asked to respond in some way, often collectively, and also often with peers they may never meet.

However, it is in the field of entertainment that collaborative working has really taken off. The most popular massively multi-player online game (MMOG) on the internet, World of Warcraft (WoW), surpassed 10 million subscribers worldwide in January 2008.[8] Players assume a role through the use of an avatar (an on-screen animated character) and can hold a number of professions, and progress from level 1 to level 60 (in the basic game), all the while taking on challenges and quests, earning money and prestige, and engaging with others.

Whereas WoW is aimed at adults, there are a number of sites for children. RuneScape[9] has a similar fantasy world, where avatars interact and work together to meet challenges. For those who prefer their fantasy through personification, Club Penguin[10] provides a flightless avatar who will waddle around playing freely with similar birds. Or you might prefer to keep a human form and visit Habbo Hotel,[11] with over 8 million unique users checking in each month.

The possibilities of online communication are extended to face-to-face meetings through the addition of a suitable camera. This can be as simple as a webcam, built into some machines, or a high-specification video-conferencing arrangement. In some instances this enables straightforward communication, as when a prisoner might appear via video link rather than being transported to court. In others it enables a process akin to interactive television. An expert gives a presentation and can be questioned during it. In schools, this would enable a number of classes to be taught by one teacher, located in a place remote from them, then directly to ask questions or make contributions to the lesson. In this way, pupils can have a learning experience not otherwise open to them.

These technologies can also bring children into the classroom when otherwise this might be impossible. James Brindley School, a hospital school in Birmingham, is spread across six sites. Here video-conferencing is used to include in lessons pupils who might be on a different site, or who are in isolation wards, allowing them virtual, if not actual, attendance.

Between 2003 and 2004, Becta conducted a review of the use of video-conferencing in the classroom, with the following findings.

- While teachers were generally unable to offer statistical evidence for performance gains, their judgements were that video conferencing impacted upon achievement positively.

- Teachers and students acknowledged powerful learning effects as a consequence of a video conferencing session.
- Video conferencing is, in the main, highly motivating to students, and improvements in pupil behaviour occur during video conferencing sessions.
- Teachers had yet to explore the potential of video conferencing and how it might affect the way that they taught.
- Video conferencing can support a shift to learner autonomy.
- Students can access other cultures, both unfamiliar and those of their home communities, enabling links and cultural identity to be formed and maintained.
- Video conferencing can enable 'authentic' experience – students hear things from 'the horse's mouth' and can respond immediately with their own questions.
- A 'real' audience means students take their participation seriously.

(Becta, 2004)

Case study – Video-conferencing between Shetland and South Africa

Historians value primary sources, first-hand evidence that students can analyse and assess and from which they can draw their own conclusions. So if you are studying South Africa and the apartheid system, how prized a resource is a conversation with a man who spent 12 years on Robben Island, whose jaw is irreparably damaged through being beaten, but who hung on to hope, spent his time profitably in gaining a Maths degree, which lead to a doctorate, and who now bears no malice. For the students at Anderson High School in Lerwick in Shetland, studying for their Advanced Scottish Highers in History, it was invaluable, believes Stewart Hay, their teacher. He feels it deepened their understanding of the subject, sharpened their perception, and probably raised their grades.

'Listening to Dr Isaacs talk about 12 years in Robben Island and his time in solitary confinement brutally treated with his jaw still damaged was so powerful', commented one student, Rachel Cleminson. The fact that Dr Isaacs was in South Africa and Stewart Hay's history class was several thousand miles away, in one of the remotest parts of the United Kingdom, made this an even more remarkable event. However, for this group of students it was not an uncommon one. Over the academic year 2003–04 they used video-conferencing every couple of weeks to link up with two South African schools, Langa High School and South Peninsula High School in Cape Town. 'It is, in fact, just one classroom with live argument and disagreement. Fairly strong views are exchanged between the group here and the group there', Stewart Hay found. On one occasion, for instance, one of his students in Shetland, talking about the early twentieth century, was interrupted by a young woman in southern Africa to make the point that 'We are living the mess you created'.

It is this type of exchange that demonstrates the immediacy of the medium that clearly made an impression in Lerwick. One student, Blair Grant, felt that 'It brings the reality of the past very directly to you. It makes more sense seeing and hearing from students in South Africa about what they think of their own history.'

The lessons were planned jointly with teachers from the South African schools. Sources and texts were agreed before the video-conference began, along with an issue or agenda to follow, and maybe additional work in preparation for the session. While this meant hard work for the staff and students, the video-conferences increased the motivation to get it done. 'We have to study hard for each of the video sessions – we can only hope it pays off' said Marie Goodlad in Shetland. For one video-conference, for example, the Scottish students prepared PowerPoint presentations about their dissertations outlining their research to date and their planned study to show their African counterparts. They also thought hard about how they could make best use of the medium. Bobby Gear, for instance, decided to use it 'to interview and discuss ideas of Afrikanerdom for my dissertation'.

The lessons were chaired by Stewart Hay, who was very at ease with the medium, working like a seasoned news anchor, raising questions, summarising points, and knowing just when to move the conversation along, or to make sure every voice is heard. He believes the medium makes talking easier: 'I think it blunts people's sensitivities. They are more likely to be direct. And that's the curious thing about this medium, it is much easier for me to be direct at a distance of a thousand miles to you than it is if I was sitting in that room. With students they are used to watching telly. What is new to them is themselves on that medium. It is a huge motivational boost when suddenly you're the living image. You're the person on the other side of that screen.' The numbing of sensitivities led to some lively discussions about power and government and totalitarian regimes. At least one Scottish student showed his dismay at the opposition to the apartheid regime, asking 'Why didn't you do more?'

In part, it is this openness that made Stewart such an advocate of video-conferencing, which the school began through the Scottish Executive Education Department's Future Learning and Teaching Project.[12] Anderson High School took it as an opportunity to widen its horizons, as the school is somewhat isolated. Lerwick is further from London than Milan in Italy is. The nearest railway station is in Bergen, Norway. Some of the 800 pupils board, travelling home only once a month because of the remoteness of their families on any of the 15 inhabited islands within the group of more than 100. The aim in using the medium was to establish a global classroom.

Stewart's enthusiasm for the project was not just fuelled by the benefits to his students; he too learnt a lot – especially from them. 'It is humbling. I have become a learner. I have to think differently. They say, "you don't do it this way". I am not always able to understand what is going on."

He understands enough, however, to know that what happens on the screen needs to be supported and reinforced by other means. As well as preparing presentations, the group also made use of email and a website to support the learning. The video-conferencing proved to be the most reliable form of communication, as it was run through the University of Cape Town (neither South African school had an internet connection), and colleagues there were not always able to find a reliable email connection or a working fax or phone.

One scenario for teaching and learning with this technology sees it as a means of bringing one teacher to many students – a way of delivering a lesson from one location into several places, giving access to otherwise unreachable expertise. This is a model that Stewart recognises, but would not wholeheartedly endorse: 'They see the potential as a means of replacing teachers. Here's the lecture, here's the information – which is one way of doing it. But I think the more ownership learners have of it the more exciting it becomes and the more you pre-empt – when the learner is at the centre of the thing as part of an international classroom. That means many teachers involved rather than fewer teachers. That's where I think it's at its best, where the world is directly inside our classrooms and learners and teachers are dynamically engaging in that.'

New opportunities bring new issues

What technology now offers us is ways of accessing information and communication for many different purposes that were previously unavailable. It gives opportunities to work individually and collaboratively, and to receive feedback instantly; to be able to create works and exhibit them without necessarily having to spend years learning skills, or to pass through a barrier of acceptance by another person, such as a literary agent or gallery owner.

And it makes this available to a vast number of people. While issues remain about the inclusiveness of ICT as a medium, it does allow individuals to choose to work and share without needing to seek accreditation and approval, although this can now come from feedback given by visitors to a website, rather than from teachers and examiners. FanFiction.net, for instance, is for admirers of works in many genres, not just books. These include games, comics, television shows, films, and the Japanese formats anime and manga. Authors write in the style of an admired author, using familiar characters but developing the plot in new directions, in many cases giving the characters a life beyond their formative years. Perhaps unsurprisingly, the works of J. K. Rowling have attracted the greatest output of fan fiction, with over 350,000 contributions to the website. Once contributions have been posted, other readers can provide feedback, leading to revisions and corrections, even down to changing the grammar. This is, of course, something that happens in classrooms deriving from the assessment and marking of teachers, but in this instance a wider audience is available – one that shares with the author an appreciation of the stories from which their own creation is derived. Because it is genuinely published, available for anyone to read across the wider world rather than just in the narrow confines of the classroom, there is a greater desire to make sure everything about it is finished correctly. Feedback comes without any prior beliefs about the writer's abilities, and no relationship has developed other than author and reader, so it is likely to be objective – an honest, personal response, rather than one focused on grades and levels. Despite this, the anonymity of the feedback can also make criticism more palatable: no-one has personal feelings of letting anyone else down, or doing something that has led to their disappointment.

However, this democratising of creativity has limitations. It is recognised that ICT contributes to raising both educational standards and life chances – but it is the poorest sections of society who are least likely to be using it to this end. Some efforts are being made to bridge this digital divide, but it remains a real problem.

Digital divide

In the spring of 2007, Jim Knight MP announced the setting up of the Home Access Task Force, to find ways of extending ICT access to every home in the country where school-age children live. An *internal* briefing paper to Becta's Board in October 2007 indicates that

> while most parents have purchased a computer and have internet access at home available to their children for learning, over 1m school age children in the UK lack access to a computer at home, and over 2m school age children cannot go on-line at home (Becta, 2007d).

Although this group was due to report a year later, action was already under way to address this issue. In May 2006, the Computers for Pupils scheme was announced. Over the following two years, £60 million was allocated directly to provide machines and internet connectivity to some of the most disadvantaged students in the country. The funding was spread as £25 million each year for equipment, and £10 million over two years for internet access. This funding was based on a formula involving secondary schools with pupils from the English electoral wards that ranked highest on the index of multiple deprivation, combined with numbers of pupils receiving free school meals. This gave an indicative number, which was then halved on the assumption that at least 50 per cent of those eligible would already have some sort of home access. It was then left to each local authority and school to determine what was provided and who would receive it. While only those in Key Stages 3 and 4 were eligible, it was assumed that in many instances this would also provide access for siblings and, more broadly, families as a whole. The declared aims of the scheme are:

> 2.1 By putting ICT into the homes of the most disadvantaged secondary pupils in the most deprived areas we aim to:
> - give these pupils the same opportunities as their peers
> - provide the conditions which can contribute towards raising educational achievement, narrowing the attainment gap and supporting progress towards their targets
> - support Personalised Learning by providing access to ICT whenever or wherever is most appropriate for learning
> - encourage the development of ICT skills appropriate to the 21st century for the pupils and their families.
>
> (CfP, 2006)

However, given the breadth of technologies ICT covers, the issue of the digital divide is more complex than simply providing online access at home through a PC. Even those without this may already have access to some technologies, such as mobile phones and games consoles. On the other hand, those with a web-connected computer may not have the skills or understanding to appreciate the possibilities and opportunities open to them.

> The digital divide may be a useful term for mobilising political resources, attention and funding, but simplifies reality, suggesting superficial solutions to complex social problems. Instead, we need a more sophisticated framework for understanding what such a divide entails, what factors mediate which side of the divide someone falls on, the consequences of being on one side or the other of such a divide, and the opportunities for education to include rather than exclude people in a digital society.
>
> (Grant, 2007)

e-Inclusion

There are some users for whom access issues are immediately obvious, but often not so readily addressed. Additional access needs may be due to a range of difficulties, from physical and sensory to cognitive and communicative. Examples of the former include the blind and hearing-impaired, as well as people with conditions such as cerebral palsy. The latter may include people with dyslexia, who find text difficult to cope with on-screen, those who use symbols instead of written words for communication, and people who may find the mechanics of communication difficult to comprehend, such as those on the autistic spectrum.

As well as resources commonly present in all operating systems, such as the Accessibility Tools in Windows – which include speech input and output, screen magnifiers and key-press modifications – there are also distinctive technologies that have developed.

One branch of this is assistive technology, which encompasses specialist hardware and software adaptations that enable people with disabilities to use ICT. This includes devices that are becoming ubiquitous, such as touchscreens, which are commonly used in retail outlets or to buy train tickets, and mouse alternatives, such as joysticks and trackerballs. Other examples of assistive technology include screen readers, whereby any visible text is automatically read aloud; magnifiers, which enlarge areas of the screen; and speech-recognition programs, which allow all functions to be activated by the user's voice.

There are also devices that give the user a voice. Known as voice output communication aids (VOCAs), these translate an input (whether through touching a screen, a keyboard, or a specialist access method such as switch scanning) into speech for those who are non-vocal. Stephen Hawking is the most famous user of such as system, and has a 'sip-and-puff' device to create the speech he wants the machine to utter.

Such additional supports are only part of the answer, however. There is also a need for some users to be supported for reasons of cognition and understanding.

Case study – Harry, an assistive technology user

Harry is 13 and lives in Tower Hamlets in the East End of London. He is in year 8 at a large, mixed comprehensive, well known for its positive approach to including all learners. He has ataxia-telangiectasia, a degenerative condition of the nervous system. It affects his coordination, speech and vision. All his movements are jerky, making reading difficult because his eyes are constantly moving. Previously he could handwrite, but now he does not have sufficient fine motor control, and he can be difficult to understand when he speaks unless the listener is attuned to him. He uses an electric wheelchair, which allows him to move around the school independently.

Harry says that it is his eyes that have the biggest impact on his learning, because although he can read well, it is difficult to keep track of where he is. Also, he sometimes finds it hard to make himself understood when talking in class and, as one of his teaching assistants, Simon, points out, 'He doesn't like repeating himself.'

Kay, Harry's mother, agrees – she believes 'He can find it hard to get his point across. He gets very frustrated and we can end up in a big argument.' She is also concerned about his motor skills and how they affect his ability to write things down for himself. 'Even with a computer,' she reports, 'he is a bit unsure.'

The laptop the school has provided for Harry travels between school and home every day. It is loaded with standard software including Microsoft Office, as well as specialist titles. One of these, The Grid, enables him to use any standard package, as well as doubling as a VOCA. The other program, Clicker 5, provides on-screen grids of vocabulary to use when writing, to speed the process up. Both are designed to work with the joystick he has been provided with, which operates in a similar way to the one he uses to guide his wheelchair. He also has a specialised keyboard, with enlarged keys, to attach to his laptop to make typing easier.

The equipment was provided on the advice of a specialist advisor provided by the local authority, who visits regularly to train and support school staff and to make sure the resources given to Harry remain the most appropriate for him.

'Happy,' is how Harry described his reaction on first receiving the laptop. Although he didn't elaborate on this, it was probably for the reasons his mum gave.

'Having my own computer at home and not fighting with my brothers to get on the internet,' is the biggest advantage Harry has found. His mum agrees, 'It gives him a lot. I thought it was an ideal solution for Harry. Not being able to hold a pencil, I thought it covered all his needs. Of an evening, it gives him something to do. His brothers go and wander off, or play a game. He can play a game on his laptop or go on MSN, chatting to his friends or his cousins. Socially, it's nice for Harry. It has made his life easier,' thinks Kay. 'The main progress is that he is not stressed out: he is not reliant on other people all the time, or when he is, he can tell them what he wants them to put down for him. You don't get bits missing from work like you used to when he was in primary.'

Whilst having more opportunities to go on the internet and socialise are seen as important, Harry has also begun to work more independently on his schoolwork. Recently he took part in a traffic survey and graphed his results in Excel; for his homework he wrote up how he went about the survey and then combined these into a report.

At school, Simon believes Harry works more independently, 'In ICT he definitely can. In English we have to be reading and spelling and writing down questions for him.' It has had a positive impact on his motivation too. 'He wants to go to the lesson. He is more enthusiastic. He doesn't have to watch what we are doing,' reports Laura. 'He said to me yesterday, "That was a good lesson." I've never heard that before.'

The biggest problem encountered has been getting teachers to provide work in an electronic format suitable for Harry to use on the machine. Some subjects, particularly English and Science, have been very good about this. Others have not provided any, despite the school setting up procedures for work to be provided either through the network or via his

USB memory key. There have also been some problems getting the software working properly, although the school's technical staff have been very responsive.

Laura, one of the teaching assistants who work with Harry, has a different perspective on the problems of using this equipment in school. 'The main issue,' she reports, 'is accessibility – where to sit in the room so that any trailing leads are not a health and safety problem, and getting a connection to the school network in places where the wireless does not reach. There are adjustable-height desks in several rooms to accommodate wheelchairs, but their whereabouts doesn't always coincide with Harry's timetable.'

It is not just in the present that this technology will have a positive effect on Harry's life. Thinking ahead, his mum sees his ability with the computer as a key skill for the future. 'Computer skills will help him. He is not going to be a carpenter or a plumber. This is the line that he goes down. He will have to have this sort of job.'

The possibilities of technology

Assistive technology is a means of providing an interface between people and computers for those who find standard devices difficult to use. Increasingly the choices for all users are growing. Touchscreens and voice activation are commonplace on many devices. For assistive technology users, though, their use is not optional, and often, even with the provision of specialist devices, their interaction with the machine can remain slow and laboured. One way to ease the situation is to try to move the point of interaction closer to the point at which commands are sent to the computer, within the user's brain. Developments in our understanding of which areas of the brain control which aspects of our bodies means that if we can hook directly into these outputs, it will be feasible to control a machine with thought alone. This is gradually becoming a real possibility.

Case study – Bringing human and machine closer together

Cyberlink[13] is a means of controlling a computer that is, literally, hands-free, moving the mouse and making selections with the power of thought. Originally developed in the early 1990s, it owes its origins in part to research undertaken for the US Air Force, particularly to do with speeding up reactions by activating devices, such as weapons systems, directly from the brain rather than waiting for the nervous system to respond.

It works through three small sensors attached to the forehead that pick up brain activity and nerve impulses, process them, and turn them into commands to control the computer. A combination of facial muscle tension, lateral eye movement and alpha brainwaves create 11 'brain fingers' that can be programmed to move the mouse or to control attached devices such as a midi-player. Users don't necessarily have to move their eyebrow, for instance – simply the thought of doing it can generate enough electrical activity for the sensor to respond. It has been implemented successfully with people with a range of conditions that severely limit their ability to voluntarily control their muscles, such as cerebral palsy and motor neurone disease. With this system, they can communicate through on-screen displays or VOCA, and operate environmental controllers, independently turning on the TV, closing the curtains or switching on the lights.

Successfully triggering the 'brain fingers' can require users to learn to control their body's state, relaxing and focusing in the same way that one might when performing yoga. In this way, the technology has made users look inward, as they would if meditating, which can have the effect of calming their involuntary movements as they work to generate an alpha brainwave to move the mouse to where they want it.

It is not easy to master, however. One user, Karl Dean, a web developer who has cerebral palsy, tried it instead of his usual head-pointer and wrote his experiences up on his website. Here he describes the process of taking control of the device through the use of his face.

> After the 5th day on the Cyberlink I decided to use a brain wave on the pong [a computer game built in to the software] for the left & right movements. After many hours of experimenting on each brain wave, I found the F6 mode to be the best for controlling the left and right movements of the bat. The F6 is an alpha wave. I discovered that if I think of something exciting the bat will move to the right and relaxing or being sad will make the bat go to the left. After many hours of practicing it does become easier to control and now I sometimes find this is easier than the eyebrow click. But it does depend on how I'm feeling. At first the F6 control was very tiring, but now not so much.
>
> (www.headpointer.co.uk)

Karl dedicated a lot of time to learning to operate the Cyberlink, and documented the process closely. He found that taking control of the computer in this way had benefits, but also side-effects.

> After an hour I would get really tired. After 2 hours, I felt tired and got headaches. Once I got carried away and spent 3 hours on it. This made me feel dizzy, like my head was spinning. I think I suffered from these side effects as I was trying too hard. Consequently my brain was overloading as it wasn't used to so much activity from the subtle facial muscle and eye movements in addition to altering my brainwaves in this kind of tense, concentrated way.

Overall, though, he found the Cyberlink less efficient than using a head-pointer, for a number of reasons, but particularly because 'most days my brainwaves were different. Some days I could do the easy labyrinth (one of the training games) under 20 seconds, but other days it took me over one or two minutes to complete. It can take a lot of concentration and it depends on how I'm feeling.' The limitation that Karl had discovered was that while the technology itself is consistent, it is the user who is not so, and these personal variations can lead to frustration and disappointment, as something that is possible one day is not so the next, particularly for those with degenerative diseases who may need to balance considerations of energy exerted against outcome achieved. But for those without an alternative means of working independently, this technology offers opportunities that are otherwise impossible, perhaps becoming 'cyborgs', human beings enhanced by hardware, plugging in their sentient selves and directly driving the machines.

Case study – Closing the feedback loop

Another attempt directly to link technology to the brain to use the effects they have on each other was the Brightstar Dyslexia Programme (Bright-starlearning.com). This was an unusual, innovative approach to helping children with this condition to develop their reading skills. The core of the programme was a somewhat unconventional approach to the problem. Originally developed from research in Israel, it was based on the idea that in people with dyslexia, three parts of the brain are not working as they should: the cerebellum, eye-tracking and neural pathways. The course aims to make these three areas more efficient. For 20 minutes twice a week for six weeks, participants sat in a darkened room, wired up to a heart monitor, doing very little except keeping a red square on a zigzag road while strings of different coloured lights drifted around the edges. On-screen paths appeared, then disappeared again, the background chan-ged, first white, then purple, and the display of light trails showed con-stantly, but not in a distracting way. Interaction for the user was limited to using one thumb on a handheld device to keep the target in place. It was uneventful. Monotonous even. Throughout the process, the heart monitor was providing a feedback loop to the computer generating the image. As the body relaxed, so the different elements of it changed the ways in which the different parts of the brain inter-reacted.

'It completely amazed me,' said one parent, Pauline Atkins, whose son Christopher went through the Brightstar Dyslexia Programme, 'How 20 minutes sitting in front of the computer playing around with the mouse can get their brain working. It is like somebody has put a spell over him and suddenly changed the child completely.'

The sessions were backed up with more traditional, one-to-one multi-sensory teaching from one of six special educational needs teachers all qualified in this field, although only once each week for 40 minutes. So over the six weeks pupils receive four hours tuition in total. Some of them made extraordinary gains in reading and spelling – improvements that were measured in years, not months. Of those who attended, 97 per cent showed improvements, with two out of three improving by more than 12 months in at least one aspect of literacy. Follow-up studies showed that these gains were sustained.

All potential students, adults and children, were tested when they first applied to ensure they could benefit from the work and to provide guidance for the tutors. This also provided a benchmark so that students could see the progress they made.

Matt Speno was one of the tutors. He was experienced in this field before he joined Brightstar, having taught in his native America. He provided a structured teaching programme and also tried to boost his clients' self-esteem. Having seen the impressive gains his students made, he is readily prepared to acknowledge the role of the technology, 'Two years three months in six weeks. I'm good but I'm not that good.'

He became very much a convert having at first been very unsure: 'I just know it works. You've got to be sceptical. But day in day out, I've seen the benefits. People reaching their true potential.'

Christopher was one of those who has benefited from Matt's dedication. He came to Brightstar when the company offered ten pupils from the local area the chance to try the programme. The effect on both his literacy skills and his self-esteem was reflected in his school performance. 'I did a PowerPoint project on dinosaurs for my interviews at secondary schools and I think that Brightstar helped me feel confident to do this. I also did some stories which my headmistress published in our school newsletter, she said she was very impressed with my imagination. I don't think I could have done that stuff last year.'

As Matt acknowledged, 'The children are getting good teaching in their schools.' However, for him the speed of change was the impressive thing, 'They are attaining things that would take time in a standard programme. It is the time, that little amount of time, that blows my mind.'

Despite its promise, Brightstar seems to be one of those innovations that fails to become established. Its British activity has stopped, so California seems to be the place to go now for those who feel it would meet their needs.

Can technology really change the way our minds work?

While Brightstar was developed to quite deliberately alter the way the user's brain works, it raises the question of whether simply using technology in our daily lives will do the same in uncontrolled, unexpected ways. Marc Prensky, a writer and thinker in the field of ICT in education (who coined the term 'digital natives' to describe today's young generation), believes there is evidence to show that it is. Writing about 'brain plasticity', his findings reinforce the theories that underpin Brightstar.

> However, brains and thinking patterns do not just change overnight. A key finding of brain plasticity research is that brains do *not* reorganize casually, easily, or arbitrarily. 'Brain reorganization takes place only when the animal pays attention to the sensory input and to the task.'[14] 'It requires very hard work.'[15] Biofeedback requires upwards of 50 sessions to produce results. ... it takes sharply focused attention to rewire a brain.[16]
>
> (Prensky, 2001: 3)

Prensky goes on to observe that such behaviour is easily observed in young people. 'Several hours a day, five days a week, sharply focused attention – does that remind you of anything? Oh, yes – video games!' (*Ibid.*, 2001) He goes on to state that the impact of this is that 'their brains are almost certainly physiologically different.'

It seems that not only can we harness the power of the machine directly to the brain to enable behaviours and actions that otherwise might be difficult, but we can also enrol the machine to change the brain. Further research will be needed to find out just how the brain will be affected by what stimuli, but Brightstar could be an example of how we will be using technology in the future.

A taxonomy of e-inclusion

There have been several ways of classifying technologies designed to support people with special educational needs, most recently by the introduction of a taxonomy of e-inclusion. Here three ways are identified in which technology supports 'e-inclusion': to train or rehearse, to assist learning and to enable learning (Abbott, 2007).

The first of these is identified with much of the software that has been used in schools, which is largely behaviourist[17] in perspective, such as multiple choice quizzes. The learning happens through repetition, and through cause-and-effect or trial-and-error. Learners are corrected when they give a wrong answer, and rewarded for getting a correct one, which reinforces the behaviour leading to the answer being remembered and repeated. While there is a place for such an approach in classrooms, it does not necessarily contribute to a rich learning environment, and exploits the possibilities of the technology to only a limited degree.

Technology that assists learning is that identified above as assistive technology. A similar category of augmentative and assistive technology is also included. This is where the resources compensate for some area of disability, whether physical or in learning, thus making it possible for users to access and engage in education. While hardware tools, such as enlarged keyboards for those with visual impairments or poor fine motor control, are included here, there are also software enhancements such as Communicate: In Print,[18] which provides symbols to match written texts, or Clicker5,[19] which gives on-screen banks of words to create them. Both of these support, among others, those who may find it difficult to deal with writing.

'Enabling learning' focuses on learning that could not happen without the medium of the technology. This tends to be about the communicative and collaborative aspects of it – the ways in which learners can share ideas and experiences and contribute to a common goal.

> In this case, the technology may be mobilised in an active role in the learning process: perhaps by asking questions, intervening in an activity or presenting interactive scenarios or simulations. This might involve the use of technologies to facilitate the creation of collaborations and communities where learners work together, an approach more often associated with social–constructivist models of learning, and engaging more specifically with learning in social contexts and learning through collaboration and interaction with other people. Crucially, however, the significant difference between this category and the other two is that it is only through the use of technology, albeit in a collaborative or supportive context, that particular learning can take place. The use of technology transforms rather than modifies the learning context.
>
> (Abbott, 2007: 13)

Case study – Podcasting to improve language skills

An example of technology being used to 'enable learning' is the use of podcasting with students who have a range of barriers to learning, including speech and language difficulties, as practised at Frank Wise School, a special school in Banbury.[20] Here, upper school students create podcasts about school or local news that are then posted on the school website.

Following a discussion about a chosen item of news, some students independently record their own version of the story, or a comment on it, while others have each sentence modelled to them by a member of the teaching staff, which they then repeat. In this instance the staff voice is edited out of the final version, leaving only the student's speech. Following this, members of the class offer a critique of each other's work, commenting on how well the recording can be understood in terms of language use, articulation, volume and content. Such feedback may ordinarily be difficult to initiate, but by providing an authentic, high-stakes outcome, students become more focused and will re-record their broadcasts when necessary. The polished end product is then posted on the school website (in a restricted-access area) to be shared with friends and family. The whole process provides a learning activity for students to work on collaboratively that focuses on communication skills, both in what is said and, crucially for some students, on how it is said.

Inclusion through social networks

While the starting point for the taxonomy is e-inclusion, in particular for those with special educational needs, how it enables learning can be applied to all pupils, making it an inclusive taxonomy. It also reflects the latest developments in technology, as exemplified by Web 2.0 and the possibilities of social networking for creative endeavours.

Much of this networking has been formalised by the development of websites such as Facebook,[21] MySpace,[22] Friends Reunited[23] and LinkedIn.[24] There are possibilities for sharing creative endeavours in Flickr, Fanfiction, YouTube and Blogger (see above); for the open and democratic nature of opinion and response through the feedback mechanisms on all these sites; and in the ability of buyers and sellers to rate each other on eBay and Amazon, or to provide reviews of products and services.

These tools are also widely exploited in higher education, where many courses are taught online, in part or in whole. While it could be argued that, for decades, institutions such as the Open University have been offering learning remote from the home base at times that suit the student, what is different here is the range of tools available, and that their use can contribute to assessment. Tasks can be set that require students to collaborate to produce an online presentation, or to contribute to an online discussion, or to keep a log of responses and reflections. These methods are facilitated by various aspects of the technology to bring about richer, socially constructed learning in a way previously enabled by face-to-face seminars and discussions, although with more flexibility in the time and method of contributions. Discussions can be asynchronous – contributions may be made at different times – or time-limited. Dialogues can be with one other, or with many others. Engagement can take place whenever and wherever students choose for it to happen. It is this level of flexibility, with this degree of choice, that is envisaged in Harnessing Technology and the current Building Schools for the Future programme.

Learning anytime, anyplace, anywhere

Under the Building Schools for the Future investment programme, some £25 billion is being made available to local authorities to rebuild or refurbish every secondary school in the country over a period of 15 years. Ten per cent of the investment is for ICT, part of which is to be invested in 'learning platforms', school portals that will allow staff to upload learning resources for pupils to access whenever appropriate. Here completed work can be submitted electronically, and even marked automatically if in a suitable format, and students can collaborate on tasks, communicate with each other and with teachers, and use readily available tools to create, respond and reflect. It is the intention to bring into schools the possibilities made available by recent innovations on the web, and to apply them to new ways of learning.

Among these possibilities are those presented by virtual worlds such as Second Life.[25] In this online environment, users create an avatar to represent themselves, then enter the computer-generated three-dimensional world and interact with others. Currently this is predominantly an adult environment, with several universities, such as the UK's Open University, setting up educational 'islands', in some senses to bring students doing distance learning closer together. However, there is a Teen Second Life area, designed to allow people under 18 to participate, and open to educationalists to use for teaching purposes.

As mentioned above, such areas for young people to interact on the web have been around for a while. Habbo Hotel started in Finland in 2000 as a social networking site, and by January 2008 had had over 38 million avatars created in 31 national communities. While it has no specific educational content or stated educative purpose, it demonstrates the degree to which young people will use and explore web-based communication tools. In other examples, such as RuneScape, players come together to pursue quests, collaborating to overcome difficulties and solve problems. Again, while it has no declared educational intentions the skills practised by players cooperating and communicating to complete tasks are the sorts of capabilities that are considered core to the economy in the twenty-first century. The number of such sites continues to grow. Club Penguin, from the Disney Corporation, is aimed at primary-age children, and uses avatars based on penguins for them to explore the environment, meet and play games.

While it is clear that young people enjoy using these social communication tools, it is not yet clear how useful they can be for teachers in schools to use for teaching and learning. One suggestion is that teachers will create learning objects – tasks, lessons and activities – from which pupils will learn while in these virtual environments. However, getting started with bringing so-called Web 2.0-type activities in to the classroom can be a straightforward, and rewarding activity, building on the kinds of tasks that are already regularly undertaken.

Case study – Blogging with primary school pupils

The practice of writing a diary in class is not at all uncommon, particularly on a Monday morning when pupils write about their personal news. What is unusual, at the moment, is when this diary entry is made in the form of a blog (weblog). One of the differences in working in this way is that entries can become interactive, allowing readers to respond, adding their own ideas, or discussing a point with the author. This interactivity extends to adding images and links from the blog to other places on the internet, making the whole thing a more dynamic, interactive creation than a written diary. Being web-based, they can provide children with a space to write that has a real audience, including classmates, parents, relatives in distant lands, and anyone else who can access the internet – and, of course, their teachers.

'Blogging seemed to make sense in terms of finding pupils' voices and finding an audience,' explained Miles Berry, who began using blogs while Deputy Head Teacher at St Ives School in Haslemere. 'It is better for them to think of the audience as defined as their classmates. The sort of thing that one would write would change because of that dynamic. My role was to nudge them in a direction of more reflection and thought. It changed my role from someone assessing, to someone actually engaging with what they are doing.'

Because of concerns about child safety on the internet, Miles began by using a 'walled garden' approach, using password protection so that only class members could access it and comment, although this included working from home. But wider access has its benefits.

'The real fun comes when you find another primary school doing the same kind of project and linking up and working collaboratively,' thinks Ewan McIntosh, formerly a modern foreign languages teacher from Musselburgh Grammar School, but who is now working full time for Learning and Teaching Scotland, supporting East Lothian Council in using what is broadly termed 'social software' throughout its schools and offices. He cites the example of the link-up between Sandaig Primary School[26] in Glasgow and Hope Primary[27] in rural Shropshire, who were both doing work on the Romans. The Scottish pupils were curious about Roman music, so searched with www.technorati.com, a specialist blog search engine, to find information. 'Hope Primary (in Shropshire) had got an expert in and sung and recorded this Roman music,' explained Ewan, which Sandaig pupils could then listen to and ask more about. 'The teachers didn't have to do anything, the kids were the ones doing it all. The kids were taking control of the learning and where it was going to go next.'

As well as classwork, blogs can be used for providing information to parents, for celebrating achievements, and can even be tied into assessment for learning by having pupils take turns to put entries in a class learning log. At West Blatchington Junior School in Hove, there are regular blog assemblies for classes to show off their work, with prizes for the best ones. They have found blogging particularly helpful for the children in their specialist autism provision, not only for passing information to parents, but also for giving pupils another means of connecting with the world and a means of self-expression.

As with all pupil use of the internet, there have to be some considerations of online safety. This is relatively straightforward because with all blogging tools, particularly those created especially for education, it is possible to put in restrictions on who can add to the blog and how responses are handled. At West Blatchington, John Mills, ICT Coordinator, reads everything his class post, and has set up an email account to receive all responses before they are added to a readers' comments page. In Scotland, Ewan McIntosh puts no restrictions on feedback, but receives an email alert whenever any is received so that he can immediately read it and delete it if necessary, 'Although most blogs get lots of positive, constructive, comments,' he finds. He also believes that because children will also be blogging in their own time, they need to be taught to do it responsibly, 'A bit like sex education.'

Although blogging is a common activity on the web, with sites such as www.blogger.com giving space to anyone who wants it, there are also spaces specifically for education. For instance, http://edublogs.org offers free facilities for anyone in education, making it fairly easy to get started. Although John Mills found that 'They are quite a scary proposition at first. When I first saw a weblog I didn't think I would have the technical ability to manage one, until I found out how easy it was.' In fact, according to Ewan McIntosh, 'It is very straightforward. If you can send an email you can blog. When you press Send on a blog, you are publishing to an audience.'

However, you may want to introduce publishing to the internet gradually, as Miles Berry did. 'We used it principally within the confines of timetabled ICT lessons. Then pupils accessed it from home – it was password protected – which brought in home learning.' Ewan McIntosh agrees that a measured start is necessary, 'At first I wouldn't start publishing directly to the web. I would begin with the teacher moderating, as kids usually prefer to have it read first before publishing. What you might want to do is make up an ID for kids to use, then they can get published, but you can check it first.' He admits that 'It needs a little investment of time in the beginning, but in the long term it becomes more pupil-led and therefore less stressful and less time-consuming for the teacher.' Ewan also believes that 'The teacher's job changes from teaching kids stuff to showing them where to go to find out for themselves.'

Computer games in education

One area where the boundaries between the use of ICT for leisure and for education have blurred has been the use of computer games in school, whether on PCs or on handheld consoles. While there may be grumbling from traditionalists about this, the use of computer games in education has backing from the top of the education system.

> Borrowing ideas from the world of interactive games, we can motivate even reluctant learners to practise complex skills and achieve much more than they would through traditional means.
>
> Ruth Kelly (then Education Secretary),
> Foreword to *Harnessing Technology* (DCSF, 2005a)

There have been many instances of the use of computer games for learning. These include commercial off-the-shelf games that provide simulated situations, such as Roller Coaster Tycoon; modifications – or mods – where established games are changed to include educational aspects; and some that have been written especially, taking the modes and mores, grammar and narratives recognisable in commercial games and harnessing them for educational ends. There are also readily available tools for children and young people, from infants onwards, to create games for themselves.

By using an aspect of digital culture that is rooted in pupils' own experiences, the learning should have a very immediate, and in some senses personal, resonance. The computer gaming industry held back for some time from becoming fully committed to the use of its products in education, as it was felt that this would not be seen as 'cool' by active players. However, it began to embrace the idea, and in 2006 published its own report into the educational opportunities offered by computer games.

Games hold out the tantalising potential of a fully personalised, responsive and enjoyable learning experience, one in which part of the pleasure lies in overcoming difficulties and challenges while experiencing the excitement of personal growth.

> They are tools for learners' own creativity and innovation. In the future, the outcome of games will no longer solely be predefined and predetermined by developers. Instead, we will see the relationship between players and games developing in a new and radically different way, where players are encouraged to both play and create their own games.
>
> Equally, pedagogical directions are leading learners towards a paradigm of personalisation through interactivity. Play has historically been acknowledged as an important part of learning, and has been present in learning environments through simulations, role plays and quizzes. As digital versions of play have evolved, interactivity-savvy entrepreneurs, professionals, academics and teachers have naturally introduced the palate of technologies afforded them by the modern world into formal and informal learning spaces.
>
> (ELSPA, 2006: 5)

Around the same time, a couple of other stakeholders in ICT innovations – Becta[28] and Futurelab[29] – were also investigating commercial off-the-shelf games in education. The former commissioned several pieces of research into the possibilities of games in education. Futurelab also did a certain amount of research, including a literature review, before starting its own project, Teaching with Games. This reported in 2006, and found, among other things, that:

> Using games in a meaningful way within lessons depended far more on the effective use of existing teaching skills than it did on the development of any new, game-related skills. Far from being sidelined, teachers were required to take a central role in scaffolding and supporting students' learning through games.
>
> (Sandford *et al.*, 2006: 4)

In other words, games do not displace teachers as a means of instruction, they complement and supplement them. A straightforward example of this is the recently released Buzz.[30] This is a quiz game where up to four teams, each with a handset, can 'buzz' to answer questions. The game has an animated questionmaster, and players answer through selecting buttons on the handset. This has now been developed for primary schools, with 3000 questions related to the National Curriculum. Questions cannot be modified or added to, so the content and format are entirely dependent on the game. Other limitations are that the handsets connect to the class computer by leads, so pupils have to sit fairly close to the interactive whiteboard, and only one person can control the handset. However, teachers can specify subject and topic, and the dynamic nature of the presentation makes what would otherwise be a straightforward revision quiz into something even more engaging.

Case study – Nintendo DS at Bishop John Robinson School

At Bishop John Robinson School in Thamesmead, south-east London, they have been using Nintendo DS handheld games consoles as a regular feature of the range of classroom activities, which has proved to be a very engaging and motivating medium.

It is first thing on a February, Monday morning and there is a level of excitement in the air that you wouldn't normally associate with Maths at this time of the day. It is a buzz punctuated by the tinny tones of Nintendo DS handheld games consoles being started up. The noise rises briefly to a peak, like a swarm of musical mosquitoes, when the class teacher Lisa Hann says, 'Everyone click on English.' As they do so, the 16 machines trill to confirm that they are initialising and connecting wirelessly to hers, the one with the games card that is coordinating them all.

Everything goes very smoothly, as this is a well-practised routine that has been happening twice a week for one and a half terms. However, the use of the machines still causes a stir. 'It is a bit of a novelty,' admits the school's ICT Coordinator Mayleen Hope, 'But it is not deterring from learning. We've had them since September and the novelty has not worn off.'

In class, everyone's eyes watch the screens as they count down 'Three, two, one,' then launch into 30 quick questions from Dr Kawashima's Brain Training. The sums aren't particularly challenging, 0+4, 1+5, 4×6, progressing to 9×9 and 7+6, but that's not the objective. Pupils are challenged, mainly in pairs, to beat their own times as they repeat the exercise three times. As an added incentive, Lisa Hann plays along too, but can't quite manage to beat Noye and Benita, the class champs, who clock up an impressive 29.21 seconds on their third go. Their screen flashes up 'Your ranking is #1 out of 16', as does each screen to show the players where they came overall, but everyone seems more concerned with their individual performance than their place overall. No-one asks 'Where did you come?'

'It is helping them to think more quickly,' explains Lisa Hann, 'The game is just a different tool. Before we would have been calling out questions.' There is still an element of more traditional methods in evidence, as between each of the three goes with the consoles, there are worksheets to complete as well. This gives everyone a chance to finish the questions on the DS, but also reinforces the expectations of pace and application to learning, as the sums are attacked with the same vigour as those on the handhelds.

'It tapped straight away into behaviour,' explains Mayleen Hope, 'We use it as a tool to bring kids into learning.' It is an approach that works across the curriculum and across the school. In year one, a group of six pupils are using the built-in Pictochat facility to beam responses back to their teacher, Sally Morris, who is helping them practise their phonemes with simple words.

They are sitting cross-legged on the floor of the computer room, DS in one hand, stylus in the other, eagerly anticipating the next spelling. 'The next one you've got is "cash",' she tells them, then pauses as each notes their answer on the screen and clicks the Send button. Every response goes not just to Sally Morris, but to all the other screens too, although none of them seems to be looking to their classmates to give the first answer before they commit, as they scribble away urgently. Once they have all beamed their attempts, the correct spelling is sent back to them for confirmation and reinforcement, with Sally Morris sounding it out for them as they read it on their screen.

The machines are used in this way only for short, intensive periods. 'We use them as a tool to bring the pupils into learning, then we put them away. They know the boundaries of use. They know when they have finished,' Mayleen Hope confirms. She also believes they have only begun to tap the possibilities, having used other elements of games, such as an activity on 3D shapes from Brain Training, and different uses for the functionality, for instance using Pictochat for group writing. Here all the pupils contributed to an initial creative pooling of thoughts before starting to write, 'Then they can scroll back through them when they are writing and can grab ideas that are usually all over the board.'

One of the advantages of the devices is that they are quite common, many of the pupils have them at home, although they are not yet encouraged to bring them in. As a hi-tech intervention in a classroom, it is a very unobtrusive, easily implemented one. One that Stuart Swann, an advisor from Greenwich, the local authority supporting the scheme, describes as 'Not quite invisible.' They are hoping to extend the project to other schools, including secondaries. With the ability to replace the game card with a web browser to connect to the internet, this could lead to easily accessible information without pupils moving from their seats. 'You could pull in resources from the school network to the table. Having a search engine on the table to use any time would be amazing,' believes Stuart Swann.

The enthusiasm for the devices is shared by the pupils too: as Noye put it, between challenges on her Nintendo, it is 'A good mixture. Having fun and learning at the same time.'

Teachers determining content

An approach that is very much about using the characteristics of computer games to engage learners with educational content is that of Altered Learning's[31] modification of Never Winter Nights. This is an established computer game that has been modified by the computing faculty at North West Notts College in Mansfield, to help students complete the Key Skills element of their courses. All students are expected to complete this component, but before the introduction of the game take-up was often only a third of any cohort. A group of lecturers changed the game so that the fights and challenges were replaced by tasks to provide evidence for the qualification. For instance, when trying to get past a monster in order to cross a bridge over a swamp, players have to punctuate a paragraph correctly rather than engage in mortal combat. The result is dropped into a text file, which is then used to compile a portfolio of work to satisfy the Key Skills requirements. While the activity is not authentic in terms of the game, students are completing and submitting evidence where once they weren't. Completion rates have risen to around 95 per cent.

Another example of a modified game is DoomEd,[32] built out of the popular game Doom. The intention is to provide a game environment with real problems to solve, with an authentic learning situation situated within it. Here players have to navigate the underground railway tunnels of London that have become contaminated with radiation. Only by choosing the correct forms of shielding for the different varieties present can they overcome the aliens and get out. Failure results in death and having to start all over again. In this game, all the information necessary about the chemistry involved is embedded within it, through information posters on the walls, for instance. As a first-person shooter, the player is very much engaged in getting out of the situation, so there is an immediacy to absorbing and using information that might not be present when taught in other ways. The early stages of the game involve learning about the situation and how to play, mainly by shooting a lot of aliens. As it progresses, so the problems are introduced, becoming progressively more difficult as the game goes on. The situation, and the learning, become very personal to the player.

In these instances, it is the game format that has enhanced and thereby enriched the learning, rather than the content of the game itself. A developing area of ICT in education is the output of games where the genre is used as a means of delivering particular learning goals. One recent example is DimensionM,[33] a multi-player online game for learning Maths. Here groups of players, often only meeting through the web, take on tasks, but to complete them they need to apply mathematical skills that they may not already have. For instance, to retrieve objects scattered around an island, they have to move to different reference points, and along the way they are tested on their understanding of positive and negative coordinates on the x and y axes. If they don't know how to do this, they have to learn the knowledge first.

Computer games offer a very personal level of engagement with learning. The progress of players, or rather learners, depends on their own abilities in resolving the problems that arise. One important quality of games is that users expect to fail. A game would not be well thought of if it could be completed immediately without any setbacks at all. Failure is expected and recognised as part of the process of learning. This is not always the case in classrooms.

> Engaging in computer games and adhering to their rules means that users have a framework in which to explore, probe, hypothesise and test. This active discovery places the learner as co-producer of knowledge, an important aspect in the Personalised Learning paradigm.
>
> (ELSPA, 2006: 14)

Not just players but creators

Not only are games being used to teach aspects of the curriculum, they have also become part of it themselves. The recently introduced Diploma in Digital Applications is a modular qualification, aimed at 16-year-olds, that includes a game-making module. A number of products have sprung up to support this emerging subject. Mission Maker from Immersive Education[34] is one such, which produces very high-quality end results. However, there are a number of free applications as well.

MIT has produced Scratch[35] as a free download that will produce simple platform games (think Super Mario Brothers and Sonic the Hedgehog), whereas Thinking Worlds[36] from Caspian Learning creates three-dimensional worlds for users to explore. These, more typically, will be used to create task- or mission-type games where players encounter avatars and have to gather information to complete the game.

What resources such as these are doing is putting into the hands of young people the means to let them become creators rather than simply consumers of this aspect of contemporary culture. They can become participants in its ongoing development, and with the ease of posting their creations on the web – just as with text and images – they can publish and share their output for others to try out and give instant feedback.

Case study – Creating computer games with primary school pupils

Marion Reilly, a primary ICT advisor in Tower Hamlets, runs classes at the City Learning Centre using innovative approaches and new resources, to teach the pupils and pass on skills to the teachers. Sometimes the response to these lessons can be very uplifting – as feedback goes, it's hard to beat a spontaneous, rousing round of applause, particularly when it comes from 10- and 11-year-olds of whom you have been making challenging demands of all day. But that is what she received after a day with a year 5–6 class who had been making maze games similar to Pacman, using Scratch, a free downloadable game-authoring software developed by MIT.

The games were simple enough in concept. A character navigates a maze, receiving points for objects collected, and returning to the start if the walls are touched or they fall foul of a monster of some sort. As well as learning about the 'control' element of the ICT curriculum, the children were also using skills from Maths for setting coordinates and variables, along with basic concepts of shape and space. Then there were the less measurable ones of critical thinking, problem-solving and collaboration, coupled with a need for patience and perseverance. As a model of a design process – creating, evaluating and testing – the feedback happens very quickly and can be quite unforgiving, as Marion explained: 'The games testing environment is very rigorous. If it doesn't work, it doesn't work.'

As the day progressed, so did the complexity of their creations. Working with Iman, Mayeen used slowly turning arrows (clock hands from the gallery of objects built into the software) as obstacles for players to get past. Elsewhere, Francesca and Maisha used a dragon and made it breathe flames when approached – touching the flames sent the player back to the start with a deduction of 6000 points.

The children also picked up the language of programming. Mayeen very quickly deciphered the drag-and-drop building blocks of code brought up on the interactive whiteboard, 'When clicked. Forever if. Goto coordinates,' he confidently recited. Among the pupils, there was a lot of talk of starting a club in school to develop the projects further, and of rushing home to download the software for themselves. As it is, they can all revisit the games, as they have been posted on the web to show off and share with family and friends.

Learning beyond the boundaries of school

The use of the internet is providing a way for new technologies to further extend the opportunities for learning beyond the school, sometimes by bringing into reach resources that otherwise would not be available, at other times by providing them in diverse situations. Many of the web's innovations have been commercially driven: as well as those previously mentioned, such as YouTube and Fanfiction, there are others with direct relevance to the classroom. Both Google Maps and Google Earth immediately support a range of subjects, particularly Geography and Development Studies. Other resources, such as link-ups to real-time cameras, may be supported by public authorities, or by charities, as with Africam.[37] However, there are instances when the development of content is unlikely to come from the commercial sector because of the cost of innovation, and because it might be for a limited audience so the investment may not be worth the return. This was part of the thinking behind the establishment of the now defunct BBC Jam site.

BBC Jam was started in 2005, when the BBC was commissioned to spend £75 million of public money to create digital online resources to help deliver the curriculum. This was to become a website of innovative curriculum resources to support teaching and learning, both in school and out. The site was closed down in 2007 after a challenge in the European courts that it was anti-competitive, and finally killed off by the Governors in February 2008. This was unfortunate, as the resources developed for pupils with special educational needs were particularly creative, and unlike anything else that had been seen so far. There is some hope, however, that the special educational needs content will emerge through other avenues. Those that had been created at the point of suspension included materials for secondary-age pupils with complex special educational needs to support field trips; materials to teach reading to the deaf; others to teach both Science and Maths to the blind; and a bank of video clips of inspirational individuals who had overcome personal problems and gone on to succeed, to raise aspirations for all those with special needs.

As an example of the content that it is hoped will re-emerge, the Field Trips section has topics such as going to the beach, the woods or the shops, supported by short video clips from everyday situations that are the kind of quality one would expect from the BBC. These are backed up by games and environments to explore.

The on-screen books for deaf pupils were designed specifically for that audience, so many users found it a bit odd that when a book opened on the screen and an animated 3D environment popped up enticingly, there was no soundtrack. However, the resources it did have included signing avatars, and books with English text, or British Sign Language, or both, as the illustrations came alive to sign the story.

The really innovative sections are those that will no doubt re-emerge. These include a sentence-creator that builds one word at a time, with an animation that changes as it does so. Change a word, 'Mum' for 'Dad', 'big' for 'small', 'key' for 'ball', and every alteration changes the illustration and animation; also 'had' for 'have', for instance, to show how tenses affect meaning. The same idea is incorporated into a script-builder with avatars that read the created text back in British Sign Language.

With the Science resources for blind pupils, everything is done through sound, with headphones providing a soundscape for children to explore, solve problems and play games. A three-dimensional environment is produced through sound alone. There are graphics running, but these are to help sighted staff supporting pupils to understand what is going on. They are completely unnecessary for completion of the activities.

One example of this is when the user finds that they are in a mine. To go further down you need to create a circuit by choosing the materials that are good conductors, hook them up to an exercise bike and power an electric motor. As you pedal away, with two fingers hitting keys on the keyboard, the bike wheel whirrs, the electric motor buzzes and your heart pounds. But you have to be careful – if you go too fast you blow the circuit and have to start again.

The soundscape is very effective. When walking through a wood, birds call, grass swishes (differently depending on its length), and a waterfall thunders. All the time, players, transformed into woodland creatures, are seeking something, whether information, food or safety from predators.

With the numeracy materials, SOS and the Big Maths Adventure, there are a series of 12 online Maths games for blind primary-age children. These tackle concepts that can be difficult to teach for this group, such as number, time, and shape and space. Again they work entirely on surround-sound, with on-screen visuals again as a sop to the sighted. Several sections include a clock that, as you move the hands, you hear the cogs ratchet around the back of your head. Chimes of differing pitches ring as the hands point to the numbers on the face. This idea is then applied to drawing shapes – within the game, this is to rebuild a town destroyed by alien invaders. To practise counting, users round up a farmer's stray cows that were scared off by the invaders, while helped by a sheepdog, counting them up as they play.

There are few resources that are so tightly targeted to meet the needs of these low-incidence special needs, to help them enjoy learning and achieve their potential, so the impact of their withdrawal has been felt more keenly than the loss of some of the other content. As an example of the potential of the internet, they show how it can deliver exactly what pupils need for learning, wherever they are.

Learning in the palm of your hand

Another example of technology enabling learning beyond the established boundaries of schools is the development of portable devices, in all their forms, that enable children and young people to carry educational materials around with them, or to engage in creative, school-focused activities wherever they are.

There are a number of ways in which such portable technology can provide information in any situation. The ease with which podcasts can now be made means that students can absorb them while sitting on the bus. Not only can teachers create these easily with programs such as Podium,[38] but they can also be generated automatically using Audio Notetaker.[39] This software will take any text file and convert it to a sound file using a digitised voice, then turn it into an MP3 file for use on any portable device capable of playing these back, whether an iPod, PDA or even a phone.

Mobile phones can also be useful in themselves for learning on the move. This is not just passive learning, some of the content can be interactive, either directly online or it can be downloaded, responded to, then returned to the originator. The BBC GCSE revision site Bitesize has freely downloadable quizzes to support revision.[40]

Other materials have been developed for PDAs. MathAmigo,[41] for instance, is designed to reinforce learning in the classroom by providing exercises on the device to complete either in class or at some other time, such as for homework. The content can be displayed on an interactive whiteboard in the same format as on the handhelds, and the system includes automated marking – although, as always, teachers need to be wary of leaving all the responsibility for this to the computer, as they may not provide the same degree of challenge to a pupil that a teacher might.

Also becoming much more common are e-books, electronic versions of texts reformatted to be more easily accessible for portable machines. These can also be created very easily by downloading an add-on for Microsoft Word called Read in Microsoft Reader.[42] There is some anecdotal evidence to suggest that, when texts are presented in this format, children who have reading difficulties – particularly boys – are more motivated to read.

Handheld devices also take learning beyond the boundaries of the classroom by providing powerful computing tools in any situation. Quite commonly they are used for data collection in places where other devices would be impractical; this could be pond-dipping, or high up on a mountain. Software such as WildKnowledge[43] is designed for such tasks. Built as a scientific key, this asks a number of questions to help identify whatever has been found – fish, fruit or fowl. Using the built-in GPS on the device, you can locate that record quite precisely to where it was created. This capability has wider applications than data collection. Pupils on field trips can record their responses to a situation by text, image or speech, or answer questions provided through the device, and have these linked to the location. On revisiting the site, their previous responses can automatically be brought back to them. Alternatively, they can be provided to others to build on further.

There are many applications for this sort of resource. By using software such as Mscape,[44] created through the Mobile Bristol project, numerous possibilities arise. One that links in well with the History curriculum is to make a trail around a local area. As users walk the route, information in any format pops up on the screen, triggered by the GPS. This can ask for a response, which is instantly recorded. Other uses might include using real locations to explore coordinates, or understanding a map better through presenting real features on a landscape.

One way in which handhelds are helping to push at the boundaries of educational activity is through allowing exploration of ways of learning to a greater degree than possible previously. Two theories of learning predominate in UK classrooms: behaviourism and constructivism. While the former is evident in many ICT resources, the latter is less so, as it focuses on the individual's construction of their own understanding, often through interaction with others. However, taking this theory of learning as a starting point, combined with the use of handhelds, one computer scientist has begun to find ways of increasing opportunities for children to learn collaboratively, and socially, in the classroom.

Eduinnova – Software based on theory

Every piece of software is underpinned, intentionally or not, by the developer's understanding of how we learn. Software that is used for drill-and-practice-type activities – answering multiple-choice questions repeatedly until you get them all correct, for instance – is behaviourist. Since the mid-1970s, interest has grown in constructivist learning, where pupils create their own internal knowledge map based on what they have discovered, often through problem-solving exercises. In order to do this, we need to work with others, to engage in conversations and exchange ideas, hence the development of a social–constructivist perspective. ICT can facilitate learning through such means in ways that have not been available previously.

Miguel Nussbaum, Professor of Computer Science at the Catholic University at Santiago, Chile, began developing his Eduinnova[45] system in the late 1990s because of his belief that education was not producing the skills necessary for the modern world – not hi-tech ones, but skills of human interaction. 'What we need in the twenty-first century is the development of social and communication abilities. What I try to foster is to bring technology to change the classroom, to develop the social and communication abilities. For me, group-work is the key.'

The device itself is also important, especially its size, although he is most excited by what it allows to happen. 'I need a seamless machine – a machine that is as transparent as possible. What I want is to make the social network the key element inside the classroom. When you have the technological network, you can support the social network.' PDAs are small enough to sit in the hand, so don't obstruct students' view of each other in the same way that a laptop might; or require a particular stance, as sitting around a desktop would. With a handheld device, the computer can almost disappear while the participants talk.

Starting with 24 schools in Chile, he has developed a system based on using handheld computers supported by a web-accessible database of over 15,000 activities covering Maths, Spanish and Science. The success of his methods is shown by the growth of international interest. Already, schools in Argentina, Brazil and the USA are adopting his ideas, along with three in Wolverhampton, and other UK schools are waiting to begin.

The learning process starts with a computer randomly assigning pupils to groups of three. Although some might consider this a risky strategy – that teachers should control grouping, taking into account respective abilities, skills and social networks – the randomness and the number are integral to the approach. 'When there are two pupils in a group, there is a conversation,' argues Nussbaum. 'With three, you have a new dynamic. When there are four, too many viewpoints appear. It is more difficult to converge.'

The randomness also means that pupils are forced into social relationships they would otherwise avoid. Nussbaum tells the story of children in Santiago who were involved in violent gangs. When the computer grouped them toge-ther, they protested, but the teacher said 'I'm sorry, the machine has put your numbers to work together, there's nothing I can do.' Despite their misgivings, they set about a task discussing a book. Later, having seen them working, she reported, astonished, to Nussbaum that 'It was impossible to think that those children would ever talk to each other – and much less about literature.' It is this use of technology to bridge social divides and facilitate learning that schools across the globe want to adopt.

In Wolverhampton, there has been pioneering work going on for some years in the use of handheld computers in the classroom. Eduinnova and its social–constructivist approach offered an exciting new way of learning with them. At Stow Heath Junior School, they have been using the software in year 6. In one lesson, the class prepared for a field trip to Tenby in south Wales.

As their handheld computer screens simultaneously flashed up 'correct', one group of three, Josh, Aaron and Jack, let out a cheer. Remarkably, their classmates ignored them – they were far too engrossed in their own learning to notice.

The three boys had just worked out why Tenby in south Wales has a wall around it. 'It can't be to stop local hoodies from vandalising the place, because it was built in medieval times and hoodies weren't around then,' said Josh. Meanwhile the other two had agreed, and they now had to work out which of the other four answers it could be. Only when all three pupils had given the same answer and wirelessly transmitted it back to the class computer would they receive the next question.

The whole program is controlled by the class teacher, in this instance Gavin Hawkins, the Assistant Head, who can use their own PDA to draw attention to one particular aspect of the lesson, or to freeze all the screens to talk to the whole class. 'On my PDA I'm getting all the answers,' he informed the class. 'Every group is getting question five wrong at least once.'

As the class lifted their heads to focus on the board, the screen from Jordan's machine came up for all to see. At the top was the question: 'Tenby is famous for being a medieval walled town. Why do you think it was important to build a wall around the town?' and then the five possible answers.

The way the Eduinnova software is designed is such that the answers are in a different order on each device. This promotes discussion, because pupils can't simply say 'The top one', or 'B' – they have to quote the whole text to each other.

'To protect the town from the Welsh' was the rather unexpected answer, which Jordan went on to explain. 'In medieval times, Tenby was owned by Henry the Eighth. It was to stop other countries from getting it.'

Gavin Hawkins then unlocked their PDAs and they settled back to work. Although the classroom looks like any other, with the exception of the banks of chargers around the room, something quite new is happening through the way in which these devices enable the pupils to learn.

The school is quietly confident of a significant improvement in Maths SATS results, although the biggest changes that have come about through the introduction of the PDAs have been less easy to measure. 'It has had a huge impact on social skills,' reported Louise Russell, whose year 5 class have had their PDAs for just four weeks. 'The effort they make to try to help each other is just incredible.'

Sarah Corey, achievement coordinator, believed that this was a direct effect of working with the software. 'With Eduinnova, the computer puts them in groups. Children from families who don't talk have to work together. I couldn't get away with doing it, but the computer gives them all a number and there is no argument.'

As well as affecting the relationships between pupils, there has been a shift in the role of the teacher, at first through just getting to know the technology. 'If they can teach me something I haven't found myself, I give them five house points,' says Corey.

This developing responsibility is also found in the children's approach to classwork. Tim Franks, the recently arrived Head, has seen 'a shift towards kids working for themselves in lessons – not the teacher having to deliver everything from the front.' It's a belief reinforced by Gavin Hawkins, who says there are occasions when 'the teacher becomes a facilitator and the child almost becomes the teacher.'

The cooperative, constructivist learning theory underpinning Eduinnova has been used elsewhere in the world at every level of education. Multiple-choice activities that lead to discussion can be perceived as just a new way of doing established activities. However, there is another element of the software, called Colpad, which offers more than that. Here learners use blank screens to address open questions.

In Stow Heath, the class is set the task of providing answers to the question: 'Why is it good to walk to school?' They begin by each scribbling down an answer. After everyone has answered independently, the class teacher uses the wireless network to put each of the group's answers on each of three PDAs. From here, the trio have to come to one response that they all agree on, or come up with a new one. Once these have been sent back to the central computer, the distillation of ideas continues, this time with each group debating perspectives that originated elsewhere in the room. The process goes on until a whole-class position is agreed, facilitated by the teacher, who can intervene to share selected thoughts, sometimes using the SynchronEyes software which monitors every device and can bring up any one of them on the whiteboard for all to see. While there may be some differences of opinion about the final statement, all the pupils will have had a chance to be heard, and a consensual position has been agreed.

In going through this process, the pupils have had to address a real-life problem, engage in higher-order thinking skills, listen to and debate other points of view, and develop their own, and the group's, ideas. The approach has wide application – Gavin Hawkins states 'I cannot think of a subject where this approach could not be used.'

e-Portfolios, digital archives to record the learning journey

As with other recent developments – photo and video sharing, sharing ideas through online diaries or blogs, and contributing to a common pool of knowledge on a wiki – much of this falls outside of traditional ways of creating and accrediting work. Rather than recognised experts (usually teachers or examiners) providing an assessment, anyone with access to the work can make a judgement, as long as a feedback mechanism is provided. This means of recognising achievement falls outside the usual syllabus and certification route, and is less easy to record on a CV.

These new ways of demonstrating learning and recording achievement are leading to new methods of storing and retrieving information. From Easter 2008, every child in state schools in England is required to have an e-portfolio space, an online repository where they can store and retrieve electronic artefacts to show others. As well as being able to upload examples of work from school in any format, including text, images, sound, video and even games, there will also be the opportunity to include work created outside school, or to link to websites where it will be available. This might be a personal site, or a public one such as Flickr, which is used for photo sharing.

Once posted, these items and links will then be available for the owner to show to interested parties over the web. It is thought there will be four possible ways in which this information will be useful:

- at the point of transition, from one learning situation to another
- for assessment – already some qualifications use these, such as some NVQ modules from the City and Guilds
- to demonstrate, reinforce and contribute to learning, either one's own or to help others
- as a tool for presentation, for instance to a prospective employer or higher education establishment.

Although in further education such portfolios have been in use for a while, their introduction to schools is comparatively new. The intention is that eventually they will be available throughout a pupil's school career, and beyond, to record their learning journey – the route they have taken to get to their present place. In some instances, the content and output will be determined by the requirements of a situation, such as for exam coursework. However, pupils will have some control over how the information is repurposed and displayed for other audiences, allowing them to demonstrate the range of skills they have that are appropriate at the time, to give a personalised account of their achievements. This could include content from within school – an essay or photo of a piece of design work – but could equally have examples from informal settings, such as a video of a drama production. Through this combination of electronic artefacts, they can show both the knowledge they have acquired and the range of skills, including those of problem-solving, team-working, empathy, and so on.

The role of e-portfolios in schools

From an interview with Bernie Zakary, Head of Curriculum and Assessment at Becta[46]

Has the target been met that all pupils will have access to an e-portfolio by spring 2008?
Yes. The target within the Harnessing Technology strategy was that by spring 2008 the relevant agencies and authorities would be in a position to provide the opportunity for all learners, of compulsory school age, to have access to this online learning space. It has been met.
Are there any up-to-date guidelines or specifications on what such an e-portfolio should be capable of?
First off, we must be careful not to think that the only way that a learner can access this facility is through something that is sold with 'e-portfolio' on the box. In order to try to make communications to schools easier to

understand, Becta is integrating e-portfolio functionality – what we expect it to do – into the wider specification of what we anticipate learning platforms would be able to do.[47] If these guidelines were to be adopted by a school adopting a learning platform, they would be confident that they had also acquired the bit of functionality that an e-portfolio can handle.

What's the point of e-portfolios? Who wants them, who will use them?

'e-Portfolio' tends to refer to digital assets that are maintained, or kept, either for or on behalf of a learner. The definition tends to focus on the individual, whether it is for assessment for summative or formative processes.

The informal e-portfolio [the use of websites such as YouTube or Flickr to show off creative endeavours] is used for social networking, to meet the individual's needs in a completely different way. Of all these different things, there is nothing cut-and-dried to say those divisions will remain, as the accepted norms of education and training change.

Is there a difference between what is needed for primary and secondary schools?

There are different emphases – yes. In the primary setting there is less emphasis on preparation for formal qualifications. I've seen interesting work done in some primary schools, where teachers get kids to choose a piece of work each week, ask for peers to comment, and then put it in a place on the network where parents have access to it. I'm not saying there is not the scope in secondary schools to do this, but as kids get older and prepare for public exams the things they can do with their e-portfolio change.

How will e-portfolios fit in with other e-learning tools, such as learning platforms?

When I go into schools now, the workplace is much more geared up to Personalised Learning approaches. The records that are kept about individual performance are much more detailed. There are products, such as learning platforms, designed specifically to do the same. They allow teachers to personalise without increasing their workload. The fact is, with digital resources it is easier to keep track of work, to annotate, to update.

Why not encourage pupils to use what's out there, such as social networking sites or blogs?

There is a natural reticence in schools to build pupils' use of this sort of social networking into the formal curriculum. It's an aversion to something teachers can't check up on.

Will an e-portfolio belong to the learner or the school?

There are no hard-and-fast answers yet. When people do A Levels and GCSEs and send off projects and scripts, they get the grade back but they don't see the work again. If I was producing stuff, I would probably have a digital copy of what I have sent saved somewhere.

Who will decide who has access to it?

Access will be given to the people for whom access is designed. Coursework will be [for] the learner, and their teachers and tutors to provide comments on progress. And there may be a chance to invite comments from other learners too. If the work is about to be signed off for assessment purposes, it probably goes into a different area of the portfolio, date-stamped, then made available to whoever is designed to have access to it in the next phase [such as examiners or moderators].

What rights might parents have in relation to their children's e-portfolios?

There is lots of research that pupils do best where there is parental involvement. Active, supportive involvement. If technology provides a way for parents to engage in that in a more meaningful way, that is only to be encouraged.

Who will be responsible for ensuring the information is accurate and truthful?

It depends on the purpose. If it is the bit [of the e-portfolio] just used for personal reflection, that is between the learner and their conscience. If it is something that is part of a formative process round a piece of work, then the main thing of interest is that it is where it needs to be and it belongs to that learner. The teacher makes sure that it belongs to the learner, just as with an exercise book.

What happens to an e-portfolio if a pupil moves school?

There is no established process for it to be packaged up in a particular way or for the receivers to use it in a particular way. There is an opportunity there for that sort of material to be capitalised on. It is about working out a way [of moving it] without swamping schools.

Kids will be savvy about the use of digital content, thinking 'I'm going to save that, or copy it to a social networking site, or put it on a memory stick.' Digital stuff is infinitely copiable. From the point of view of the learner, this might not even be an issue.

What happens to an e-portfolio once a student leaves school?

You have the ability for candidates going to university to submit stuff to UCAS. With coursework they are permitted to keep copies, and do. Submitted work belongs to the awarding body. What will emerge is digital equivalents of what is currently acceptable.

In the end it will be about the purpose. It will be built into the design of the e-portfolio.

There is a powerful argument for e-portfolios for lifelong learning and for assessment. It is an irony that technology has such great power for learners, with a variety of disabilities, but technology built into assessment can make it more difficult for one group or another [to hold onto their work].

ICT can help us to know students better

Technology offers opportunities for young people not only to present themselves to the world, but also to gain insights into their individual, psychological make-up – useful for both themselves and their teachers.

Over the past 20 years, understanding of how the brain works, and therefore how we learn, has developed considerably. One aspect of this has been the growth of interest in learning styles and in 'multiple intelligences'.

The first of these suggests that we all have preferences about how we like to learn – the guidance in English schools through the National Strategies has been that we have three such styles: visual, aural and kinaesthetic (VAK) – through seeing, hearing and doing. Although just what constitutes a learning style, and how we identify them, is the cause of considerable debate, Melis and Monthienvichienchai (2004) quote one study that suggests there are 69 identified learning styles.

However, the National Strategies keep it manageable, and many of the training materials for Key Stage 3 include information on VAK. For instance, *The School Library and the Key Stage 3 National Strategy* (a course for librarians) describes each of the styles in the following ways.

A visual learner:
- prefers to read, to see the words, illustrations and diagrams
- talks quite fast, using lots of images
- memorises by writing repeatedly
- when inactive, looks around, doodles or watches something
- when starting to understand something says 'that looks right'
- is most distracted by untidiness.

An auditory learner:
- likes to be told, to listen to the teacher, to talk it out
- talks fluently, in a logical order, and with few hesitations
- memorises by repeating words aloud
- when inactive, talks to self or others
- when starting to understand something says, 'that sounds right'
- is most distracted by noises.

A kinaesthetic learner:
- likes to get involved, hands on, to try it out
- uses lots of hand movements
- talks about actions and feelings; speaks more slowly
- memorises by doing something repeatedly
- when inactive, fidgets, walks around
- when starting to understand something, says 'that feels right'
- is most distracted by movement or physical disturbance.

(DfES, 2004b)

Although there are three learning styles here, the distribution of these pre-ferences across the population is not even. The same publication points out that 'Research indicates that in general 35 per cent of people are mainly visual learners, 40 per cent of people are mainly kinaesthetic and only 25 per cent are mainly auditory.' (*Ibid.*)

In some ways, this could be considered a somewhat crude analysis, as quite often we are using more than one style simultaneously, and there are some things that lend themselves to a particular way of learning. For instance, learning to speak a foreign language requires an emphasis on the aural, while getting to grips with overarm bowling in cricket requires kinaesthetic input. A student will probably watch a demonstration of bowling and hear it described, but will only really learn it once they have a go. The reality in classrooms is that teachers need to use a variety of teaching methods if they are to reach all their pupils effectively.

> It is difficult to say how many learners will have a very strong preference for just one modality [visual, aural or kinaesthetic] – and, as with learning style tests in general, there is the issue of the accuracy and reliability of measuring a learner's preferences. So it is perhaps not surprising that Coffield *et al.* (2004) found no evidence that matching instruction to an individual's sensory or perceptual strengths and weaknesses is any more effective than designing content-appropriate forms of presentation and response. It may be, therefore, that matching presentation with the nature of the subject matter is both more important and more achievable than matching individual preferences.
>
> (Becta, 2006c)

ICT can help support a varied delivery of a subject, whether it is intended to teach to an individual's preferred learning style, or in a way that is most appropriate to the content. 'Representing knowledge in multiple formats does appear to result in learning gains – however, it is at least as effective to match the presentation of content to the nature of the subject matter as it is to match it to individual learning styles.' (*Ibid.*)

Despite uncertainty about the efficacy of determining and working with learning styles, the guidance does note that 'An awareness of learning styles theories may help to develop metacognition and the ability to learn how to learn.' There are a number of online materials for helping students to determine what their preferred learning style is[48] and therefore how they best like to be taught (although teachers may favour the style that best suits themselves). If teachers wish to teach more broadly to the range of learning styles their students apparently have, there are a number of attributes of ICT that can support them in the classroom. Large-screen displays, whether an interactive whiteboard or simply a projected screen, give a visual input. Adding sound to a presentation supports aural learners. And asking pupils to interact in some way supports kinaesthetic learners – for instance, showing written phonemes on-screen, having them sounded out, then sorted or moved around involves the three predominant learning styles.

Case study – Teaching ICT to pupils with special educational needs

Within the ICT curriculum are many concepts that can be difficult for pupils with special educational needs to grasp. One way to get these across is to start from a concrete experience and move to the abstract, using a range of learning experiences and sensory inputs. By guiding pupils along the way, we can help them to make the necessary connections to learn. Working in this way, with groups of pupils and exercises designed to promote discussion and use of appropriate language, they can construct their own understanding.

This example is of a group for pupils with Down syndrome in Tower Hamlets who came together every week for a term. They were from all years and several schools, mostly mainstream primaries, with only one pupil placed in a special school. Across the group there were a range of abilities, despite having a shared condition. The group ran in a similar way each week, to present a consistent framework for learning, so that pupils could move progressively forward through fresh challenges, but with the security of some familiarity.

In their school these pupils are usually the only child with Down syndrome, which is one reason for the group's existence, to bring the children together so that they can meet other pupils just like them. It is a peer group that is not normally available to them in their schools. While the policy of inclusion encourages the placement of pupils with a range of special educational needs in mainstream schools, it can result in the situation where they are themselves exclusive, the only child with their experiences and particular perspective on them.

Bringing them together had positive effects, as shown when two of the girls first met. Moryam saw Mina, pointed at her and said with a big grin 'It's me'. The emphasis on group work not only provides opportunities for socialisation, but also has an underpinning in social–constructivist educational theory.

Each week different, familiar things were chosen to talk about, looking at the concepts of similar and dissimilar as a basis for sorting and categorising. Circle-work techniques were used to encourage self-confidence and to ensure everyone had an opportunity to speak. This involved a similar introduction session at the start, which was followed by a reading of *The Very Hungry Caterpillar*. After this, each child was asked in turn to remember something the caterpillar ate. As they made their contributions, the teacher recorded them on the interactive whiteboard, for instance a lollipop would be drawn and labelled, followed by an apple. This was then used as the model for the first ICT task, drawing what they remembered for themselves (using 2Paint from the 2Simple Infant Video Toolkit). Working in this way, the pupils first heard the ideas, then saw them drawn, then drew them themselves.

In most instances they needed the support of a teaching assistant to complete a drawing. Some, although not all, used assistive technology tools. Jenni, for instance, used a touchscreen, which prompted Mina to try to do the same by prodding the screen, even though she is comfortable with the on-screen cursor and using a tracker ball (a mouse alternative consisting of a large ball in a stable mounting that is moved with the fingers – like turning a mouse upside-down). Once it had been printed, the group showed their work off and received appropriate praise and feedback, then moved on to the data-handling exercise.

The second part of the lesson was devoted to sorting objects. Different categories were used each week, including flowers, chocolates and fruits. Using this range of objects meant that as well as visual aspects, such as colour, pupils and staff could also use smell, taste and texture to explore the items. In this example, the group worked with biscuits. This was a problem for Abdul, who doesn't like biscuits and much prefers salad. However, as he had remembered from previous weeks the way the lesson progressed, he was prepared to play along. He chose the breadstick as his 'best biscuit' even though he hadn't tried any of them. The rest of the group, teachers, pupils and teaching assistants, also made their choices from the four on offer – an oblong chocolate bourbon biscuit; a similarly oblong pink wafer; a round, golden, cheddar cheese-flavoured, savoury biscuit; and a long, thin breadstick. It was important that the biscuits offered differed in shape, colour and taste so that the children could make their choice by any of those characteristics.

The biscuit samples were on four plates on a large table, which the group sat around. As well as these, there were also four A4 laminated photos of the choices available. As the teacher passed each plate around the group, she described them carefully by their characteristics, mentioning colour, shape and taste, and using Makaton signing to illustrate what she said.

After sampling the biscuits, the group took turns to take from the plate one they had chosen as a favourite, and place it on top of its photo. This made a very literal, concrete pictogram of everyone's choice of best biscuit, the act of moving the biscuits from the plate to the graph, of physically sorting them, providing a kinaesthetic learning opportunity. From creating this graph on the table, the children moved on to drawing one on-screen.

This was done using the interactive whiteboard. In turn, the children got up from the table, counted a column of biscuits, then moved to the board to input the data. This was made easier by the same images of the biscuits on the table being used for the categories at the bottom of each column. Having counted five breadsticks, for instance, Abdul could find the same image on-screen and tap it five times, with the whole group counting out loud as he did so. On each tap, the bar chart would grow taller by one biscuit. Abdul needed some reassurance, and after each number he lifted his head to check. He got to five, without missing out four as he often did, and waved his fingers in the air to celebrate.

Once the graph was completed on the board, the children and their supporting staff returned to their individual machines and recreated it themselves, labelling it with their own name and a title such as 'Jamal's Best Biscuits'. The exercise saw them move in steps from choosing a biscuit as a favourite by taste, colour, shape or a combination, then moving them into lines to express a preference, reproducing this on the interactive whiteboard by getting up, counting a row then tapping out the number, and finally moving to the entirely abstract task of producing a bar chart on-screen.

The final activity built on this. Photos were taken with a digital camera of the pupils posing with their choice of biscuit. These were dropped into MSPublisher, a caption added, such as 'Mohamed likes pink wafers', and the photo printed out.

In the final group session, they first discussed the data on their graphs, deciding which biscuit most people preferred, and which least. Then they all showed off their morning's work, their drawings and their photos, saying something about what they had learned and receiving applause from the others as a means of reinforcement. Back at school, the work continued in the creation of a record book with the teaching staff, using the printouts and adding their own captions. The books were then used as a basis for conversations with their friends and teachers, describing what they had been up to, and further reinforcing the vocabulary, Maths and ICT skills they had used.

Working with multiple intelligences

Beyond the idea of how we prefer to learn is also that of the differences in our individual intelligences. The development of interest in multiple intelligences has risen over the past 20 years to suggest that we each have a range of ways in which our brains work, but that it is only in the area of academic achievement that this is usually measured and accredited in schools. It is suggested that if we recognise the range of intelligences each student has, then we can find other ways of helping them both to learn and to demonstrate their learning.

This view of human intelligence is largely associated with Howard Gardner, who has been working in this field since the mid-1970s. Originally he postulated that there were seven intelligences: linguistic, logical-mathematical, musical, bodily-kinaesthetic, spatial, interpersonal and intrapersonal. More recently, naturalistic has been added to the list, perhaps because of the rise of awareness of green or environmental issues, and there is continuing discussion about whether other intelligences should also be added, including spiritual, existential and moral. (Debate continues around whether these meet the criteria.[49])

As with learning styles, online tools are available to determine which intelligences predominate in an individual.[50] If students are able to understand their own learning abilities, they are better equipped to be involved in decisions about the content and delivery of the curriculum, key aspects of Personalised Learning.

ICT as a tool for analysis

Another way in which ICT can help to ensure pupils' learning experiences are better suited to their individual needs is as a tool for assessing and analysing those needs. The degree of complexity of these, and the degree to which they suggest they can provide insights into pupil's psychological functioning, vary considerably.

Some are simply on-screen checklists, variations of paper-based products that are presented differently and then provided with some sort of electronic output for viewing the results that helps to automate the process. An example of this would be Emotional Literacy: Assessment and Intervention,[51] which provides a set of questionnaires to be completed from three different perspectives: pupil, parent/carer and teacher. These are done on-screen; or the results from a paper version can be entered, then analysed to suggest areas of strength and concerns in categories such as 'self-awareness'. The process also produces ideas for ways of working with the pupil given any particular outcomes. The advantage of having electronic versions of tools like this is twofold. Its presentation may be more engaging than a list of questions on a sheet of paper; and the analysis of the results can be supported in several ways – they can be completed more quickly, interrogated in different ways, and presented in a variety of formats. The additional link to activities provides a starting point for what to do next.

However, the use of an electronic format can also provide developers with opportunities for presentation that would not be available by other means. The Cognitive Profiling System[52] uses this facility to screen young children for dyslexic tendencies. While this company now has a catalogue of products for all ages, the original program was created with the idea of identifying children who would find reading difficult, even before they had begun to try to read. Developed by Chris Singleton of Hull University, it uses a particular model of dyslexia based on cognitive functioning. By presenting pupils with a number of activities, the intention is to evaluate their functioning across five key areas: phonological awareness; phoneme distribution; auditory short-term memory; visual short-term memory; visual and verbal sequencing.

The assessment consists of a number of activities that isolate elements of the reading process. For instance, to test visual short-term memory, children are presented with a screen where a number of rabbits pop out of burrows. They then have to replicate the order in which this happened. Another segment asks them to associate sounds with symbols – just as when reading – although without these being known phonemes (letters and their associated sounds). Abstract symbols are used with simple sounds not found in English.

The belief is that by discovering problems before starting the process of learning to read, pupils can be given appropriate support before any impediments emerge. We can know who will find it difficult before they begin, and therefore who may be vulnerable to possible difficulties.

A lot of research went into the development of this system, and it works to a particular model of dyslexia. While it is undoubtedly useful, it has an error margin of about 4 per cent, with both false negatives and false positives, that is, it will suggest some pupils have difficulties who don't – and some who do won't be picked up. There is also a need for skill in interpreting the results. While the screening process might find a problem with short-term visual memory skills, this does not necessarily mean that a narrow focus on teaching pupils to remember more accurately will resolve the issue. The outputs need to be seen in the context of developing literacy skills. So the learning of any particular skill needs to be within a teaching programme to address both reading and the underlying skill.

Another screening tool based on brain-based research is Neethling Brain Instruments.[53] This is grounded in the principle of the brain having two hemispheres – left and right – that have distinct functions, and that are each then split further to make four quadrants. By assessing in which areas of the brain students are strongest, they can be supported to use these for learning, and to develop other areas. The screening takes the form of a computer-based questionnaire that then provides a profile of their various capacities. Armed with this information, students are better able to understand their personal learning processes, and their teachers can work with them to optimise their learning. One of the issues that may arise is if teachers teach to particular aspects of the brain and miss out others, to the detriment of the pupil's learning abilities.

At King Harold School in Waltham Abbey, Essex, the profiling system is also used to support careers guidance. Students' individual profiles are compared with those of particular professions. A database of an array of jobs has been developed to create optimal profiles for each of these. Students' profiles are then compared with these to help them decide whether their aspirations are appropriate, how difficult it may be to join a particular profession, and whether they need to reassess their choices.

A simpler tool to support individuals' reflection and thinking is WaysForward.[54] This online program uses the structure, techniques and theory of solution-focused brief therapy to help them think through problems. While not intending to replace the traditional relationship between counsellor and client, it may supplement this, or provide non-professionals with access to a useful technique for helping a process of reflection and discussion. It could even be used by an individual to think through a particular issue without ever involving others.

Computer-based resources are providing us with additional ways of gaining insight into our cognitive and emotional functioning; however, they have yet to replicate the rich source of knowing and understanding that comes from human relationships. What they offer is an enhanced level of personal awareness, with which individuals can take more control over their actions and decisions – in this instance, for how and what they learn, and what educational path they choose to follow. However, we need to remain circumspect about the degree to which we rely on the prognoses of machines – they are effectively computing data to the algorithms with which they were programmed. Data can be inaccurate and interpretations flawed. We are still some distance from a time when a machine might replicate human empathy, insight and understanding.

Computers as teachers

Just as we may question the limits of a computer's ability to assess, we may also need to consider whether one can actually teach. Undoubtedly, we can learn from them, from the wealth of text, video and experiences that we are presented with. However, teaching requires an element of intervention, of mediation. What they currently will do, by monitoring answers to on-screen questions, is present appropriate material deemed to be within the pupils' range or to be stretching them further.

Some systems will provide an on-screen assessment; then set out the programme of study a student will follow; determining from the answers given whether or not they understand the content; extrapolating from this how far along the learning path they have progressed; and putting the next question accordingly. These 'integrated learning systems' also provide a range of reports so that teachers can follow progress.

Integrated learning systems were the subject of a three-year study commissioned by Becta, which resulted in a guide to good practice. This noted that 'The design of current integrated learning systems products is grounded firmly in the behavioural school of learning theory.' It goes on to say:

> Some authors claim that the construction and availability of shared understanding is central to the appropriation of new knowledge ... The behaviourist approach taken by integrated learning systems designers precludes any element of social interaction since the system is designed for use by isolated individuals often wearing headphones.
>
> (McFarlane, 1999: 20)

Probably the most widely used of these programs is SuccessMaker, distributed in the UK by Research Machines.[55] Such a system of providing questions tailored to a particular student can be said to be individualised rather than Personalised Learning. That is, the content is considered by the developers of the system to be suitable for that student, but there is no ownership offered to them of that content, no control of how or what they are learning, and no assessment for learning. They remain passive recipients of education rather than engaged and involved, proactive participants.

Tracking and monitoring

Although we might dispute whether computers can teach, as opposed to providing learning objects and opportunities, they undoubtedly have a role in monitoring and tracking. While much of this is in providing information and reports for people to act on, they can also respond automatically.

Truancy Call[56] is a system that links into the attendance registration system to send a text message automatically to a parent's mobile phone should a child fail to register. As many secondary school registers are taken electronically, even with swipe cards, this whole process can happen without the intervention of school staff, whose efforts can go into resolving whatever issues are causing the problem, rather than into checking registers and making phone calls.

While attendance is important, what is more so is what happens when pupils arrive at school. Technology can help us track not only pupils' presence, but also their achievement. There are a number of commercial management information systems available from companies such as Capita,[57] which offer packages that will manage every aspect of school life electronically. This will include tracking assessments and offering online learning resources. Latest developments in such packages also give the opportunity for parents to access their offspring's school records directly, so they know how well they are doing in school without having to wait for parents' evenings and school reports.

Such real-time reporting has yet to become widespread in schools. However, one system is used by all state schools, as it is the tool Ofsted uses to consider pupil performance and achievement. As noted in Chapter One, RAISEonline (Reporting and Analysis for Improvement through School Self-Evaluation, www.raiseonline.org) is an online system that brings together two analysis tools to give greater granularity when reviewing school data.

Previously the Performance and Achievement (PANDA) report showed schools how they were doing compared with other, similar schools across the country. Aligned with this, the Pupil Achievement Tracker (PAT) showed pupils' progression over time through their SATs results. RAISEonline combines these so that schools can interrogate the data from the level of whole school or cohort performance to an individual pupil's answer to a particular question on a SAT.

The data are loaded centrally, but schools can download the system and add to it to give it more depth, and as pupils progress through different schools it follows them to give a longitudinal, statistical view of their career, allowing questions to be raised about any particular blips, peaks and troughs within it. It allows for analysis at group and individual levels, from the extremes of the performance of the whole school, or specific cohorts, to the performance of an individual on a particular question in a given assessment. It is the tool that Ofsted now uses to evaluate a school's performance.

The whole system is framed with a number of items that provide an environment of 'contextual value-added'. This includes indicators such as pupil mobility, numbers on free school meals, and the range of special educational needs. As data build up, the path for progression taken by any group or individual can be tracked from when they entered primary school through to when they leave secondary school, and shared between schools across the point of transition. While reliance on end of key stage data may give a regular, if sporadic, picture, it does give schools a starting point to pick up inconsistencies and to interrogate the information further, thereby trying to ensure that pupils reach the Every Child Matters outcome of 'enjoy and achieve'.

Another means of sharing information, and of meeting another of the five outcomes – 'staying safe' – is ContactPoint[58] (see Chapter One). This is a database of basic information about every child in England from birth until the age of 18, that contains date of birth, address, GP, education setting, and person acting in a parental capacity. It will also have a unique identifying number. The system is expected to be in place by the spring of 2009. While this database will not hold information about assessments, or personal details such as exam results or medical records, there will be a facility for professionals to flag up that they have an involvement with, or information about, a child should others wish to contact them. As discussed in Chapter One, there will be a number of security conditions put in place, as an estimated 300,000 people may be given access to the data. They will all have been trained and given a username and password, as well as a physical token of some sort (probably a USB stick) and will have to log a reason every time they access a record.

The use of electronic data systems to keep children safe is also evident in the Lost Pupils Database. This is a means of local authorities recording any pupil who has left one of their schools but for whom there is no known destination. Other authorities can access this list if a child turns up, to find the appropriate educational records.

Conclusion

ICT offers opportunities to do what we have always done to protect and educate children more easily, and also allows us to do things that have not been possible before. It supports and develops ways of teaching and learning, offering opportunities that have not previously been available. Tools of analysis and assessment give everyone better insights into how children learn, and their cognitive functioning. This can be mapped onto programmes of work to better target the areas that need support, and to exploit their strengths. We can also engage in deeper, long-term monitoring of progress, which feeds into our assessment and analysis, thereby offering more opportunities for greate personalisation. Tracking, monitoring and information-sharing facilities also enable professionals to help children to 'stay safe' and 'be healthy', knowing where they are, what services they are accessing, who is involved with them and even, as we see in the next chapter, collaborating on case management.

ICT also offers ways of teaching and learning that can transform children's educational experiences, not only making it more personal and allowing them to develop more broadly, socially as well as academically, but also opening up the possibilities for creativity, raising aspirations and making connections. To achieve this shift requires a clear focus, leadership and determination. Given these, schools of the future can be very different places – and in some countries they already are.

Case Study – A vision of the future, now

The slogan that dominates the entrance hall of School Number 50 in Beijing, China demonstrates the country's commitment to the future, and its route to getting there. 'Technology will make this country powerful,' it declares, confidently. It is a belief that is very much in evidence throughout the institution.

Sometimes the commitment is awe-inspiring. When you walk into a darkened classroom and one wall is completely taken up by a 15-metre-wide, three-metre-high, curved screen filled with a life-size, 3D image of the Forbidden City, it can leave you speechless. This school is the city's leading 'Vocational and Technical School of Commerce and Trade' for 15–19-year-olds. It is helping to prepare China for the forthcoming Olympics, and for the future beyond that. They know they will need large numbers of tour guides, and in order to let them practise without having to traipse around all the national monuments, they have invested in this very impressive piece of technology. Students practise their patter by flying through the virtual reality environment (you have to wear 3D glasses to see it properly), giving a realistic, real-time commentary as they do so. A click of a button, and viewers are being guided through the Temple of Heaven, another click and it's the Summer Palace, complete with birds and butterflies fluttering out of the screen.

In the next room are detailed scale models of these same monuments for further orientation, complete with video screens running real footage and indicator lights on the model, so you know where you are and what it looks like. To the side of the room are information kiosks so students can bone up not just on the monuments, but also on their national history and on world geography, to connect better with their visitors.

This is not the only area where impressive investment has been made to gear up for the future. On other floors of the building are a tea shop, where young women learn the intricacies of the traditional ceremony; a glass-fronted hotel suite, with seven additional beds for potential chamber maids to practise on; a half-size, mocked-up supermarket, with every variation of till to be found in the country; a banking hall, with three different layouts for training tellers; a stock exchange, showing world trading as it happens; a CCTV control room to train security staff; an e-business suite for budding online entrepreneurs; and a room full of industry-standard editing set-ups for the television trainees.

It is all part of a government strategy, explains the college Principal Zhang Xiang Yong, waving his cigarette across the conference table to illustrate the point. The intention is to shift the balance of employment between the service and manufacturing sectors from the 2006 ratio of 30:70 per cent to a reversal of that situation by 2010. Hence the heavy investment in preparing students for work in every aspect of the service sector. Many of them will be training for jobs that don't exist – yet – but when the visitors arrive, or the western corporations, China will be prepared with a well trained workforce.

While it might sound ambitious, there is an assured confidence in these discussions. Individual pupils, like those at Niu Lanshan on the outskirts of the city, also have it. This is a school for the academic elite. Every pupil here goes on to university, the school is just another step on the way to fulfilling their ambitions. When they calmly explain in perfect English that they will be not just scientists and doctors, but politicians, diplomats and chairs of big corporations, you somehow know they will.

They are prepared to work hard to get there, putting in long hours and giving up their weekends. There are plenty of materials to learn from. Not only do the staff load the school intranet with readings and exercises, but they also use the extensive internal television system. Many of the classrooms have cameras, so that an expert teacher in one can be multicast to many others. Lessons can be recorded to add to the archive for students to revise from later. With more than 2000 pupils, it can be difficult to bring everyone together (apart from the morning exercises, when playgrounds everywhere become a mass of coordinated movement, like aerobics but to martial music). So schools have TV studios, proper ones with chroma key backgrounds, lighting rigs, a couple of cameras and a director's gallery. Even the junior schools.

While they are online, students might also look up the reading materials, simulations and exercises their teachers have created for them. They might even join in the discussion forums, as they do at Number 50 school. Here students regularly share their views in web-based forums. There are no issues of moderating the discussions, or of students abusing this tool; they are too focused on what they, and their country, are trying to achieve, to even consider going off task. 'Our students can know more about our historical culture. They have many, many fierce discussions about cultural points, and we can use this after-class material in our lessons,' explains Miss Vey, their Chinese language teacher.

As well as providing the hardware, there has been extensive investment in training. Miss Vey, in common with her colleagues, has had to take a test to show her competence with common ICT tools. She, like several others, is also learning to use Flash to create her own materials, particularly for Science, providing a skill level for classroom teachers that is a long way ahead of the vast majority of her British contemporaries.

While British schools and local authorities are writing vision statements and change-management programmes for their institutions and localities, China has gone one better and implemented a strategy for the whole country, not just harnessing technology, but making it the engine of change.

Chapter 3

A web of support

The crux of the Every Child Matters agenda is to provide all-round support for children that ensures they have access to the full range of services they need in order to thrive. This includes both universal services, such as a school place and a GP, and more specialist ones, such as speech therapy, a social worker or additional support in class. Viewing the child more holistically means that the range of practitioners involved with a child is able to take a wider perspective when working with them, as well as coming from their own narrower specialism. In order to do this effectively, professionals and staff in a number of situations need to have access to the information that the others have – not necessarily all of it, but to be able to share what, in their professional judgement, is appropriate.

There is also a desire to promote social inclusion, to reach out to children and young people who can be difficult to reach, those who are on the periphery of society and are at risk of not being in a position to enjoy and achieve, make a positive contribution, or achieve economic well-being.

Then there is the recognition of the value of early intervention, of early identification and intervention for those who might be thought vulnerable in some way, to try to give support that will prevent a situation from worsening, and to remedy it before more intensive intervention is required.

All these key activities can be supported through technology – in particular through the connectivity and functionality offered by the internet. These make it easier to work collaboratively across agencies and locations; to share information and keep others informed; to reach out to those who have become disconnected from their local provisions; and to recognise needs and step in to ameliorate them at the earliest opportunity. This chapter considers the ways in which the connectedness of ICT helps to make these outcomes a reality.

Knowing them all

Section 12 of the 2004 Children Act gave the Secretary of State for Education the right to set up databases, or require others to do so, to support the preceding sections, those headed, 'Co-operation to improve well-being', and

'Arrangements to safeguard and promote welfare'. While the information to be gathered, stored and made available is fairly generic – name, date of birth, address, gender, education and medical services, and a unique identifier – and not particularly sensitive, it has proved quite contentious. The intention of this provision of the Act is to ensure every child has access to the universal services to which they have a right, but it also allows for the immediate transfer of information if a child relocates to another provision or authority. Critically, though, additional flags can be added to records for professionals working with a child, to show that they are involved and that they may have information that is important to others. The intention of these is to promote a more joined-up working approach, by quickly showing who else is involved with a child, rather than having to ask around, or finding out by accident.

There was considerable debate about how such a system should be put into practice. Essentially there were two choices: a database that is implemented nationally and then administered locally; or a requirement for each local authority to set up its own database that could then be coordinated nationally by ensuring that they all had the same core functionality. At first the government was reluctant to opt for a national approach, given the difficulties and controversy that had surrounded previous such projects, such as those for air traffic control and ambulance despatch. Eventually, however, the national approach was adopted, and in December 2005 it was announced that it would be implemented during 2008, currently the latter part of it, and more likely early 2009.

Understandably, considerable concerns have been raised about access to the system, known as ContactPoint, which will contain a wealth of information about young people, particularly as it flags up those who are considered vulnerable in some way. The intention is to restrict access to just key staff in each service, rather than making it available to all professionals. This may include teachers with pastoral responsibilities, such as heads of year; social work practitioners; community nurses; and youth offending teams (although this still may total more than 300,000 people). As discussed in previous chapters, security measures include extensive training and a physical token, as well as a password. Staff will need to record a reason whenever they access a record.[1]

Despite these safeguards, concerns remain. The main one being that it will have a negative impact, distracting professionals from identifying real concerns by providing an overload of information that they have neither the time nor the skills to deal with.

> On balance, the database is likely to do more harm than good because it will absorb substantial money and professional time, while distracting attention away from the more fundamental problems of improving the skills of the workforce.
>
> (Evidence to the Education and Skills Select committee from
> Eileen Munro, Reader in Social Policy at the LSE,
> quoted in *The Guardian*, 24 January 2005)

The sentiment was reinforced by Richard Thomas, the Information Commissioner, in his evidence to the same committee a few days later. As the database would replace the existing Child Protection Register (which lists only those deemed to be at risk following a Social Services assessment) with one containing the details of all children from birth to 18 years, there are concerns that those in need of some form of protection might be overlooked.

> Richard Thomas told the Select Committee it could prove extremely difficult to spot those at risk of serious harm in a database covering 11 million children. Mr Thomas, the Information Commissioner, said: 'If you are looking for a needle in a haystack I am not sure it is wise to make the haystack even bigger.'
>
> (Quoted in *Guardian Society*, 18 February 2005)

Concerns raised have also focused on the security of the information – in the first instance because of an announcement in summer 2006 that the children of celebrities (an undefined category) would have their details masked, leading critics to question why the system would not be considered secure enough for that group when it is for all other children.

The security issue was again raised in autumn 2007, following a number of well publicised data losses, including two CDs containing personal details for half a million people. This led to a review of security by the consultants Deloitte, who advised unspecified modifications leading to a probable five-month delay.

Despite criticism, the project has not been cancelled, only delayed, leading eventually to records for 11 million children being available to an estimated 330,000 key staff. It is the size of the venture, and the belief that information on children and young people should be held only when there are concerns, rather than just in case concerns arise, that is the crux of the opposition of Action on Rights for Children, who have posted their concerns on YouTube,[2] citing arguments of lack of focus, diverting resources, and issues of privacy.

As a means of delivering the Every Child Matters agenda, ContactPoint is seen as providing some of the protective support necessary, keeping children safe and healthy. Although, given the more holistic view encouraged by the programme, it can also be argued that they are more likely to both enjoy and achieve if they are safe and healthy.

When universal services are not enough

When it becomes evident that a child needs more help and support than that universally available, such as a school place or access to regular medication, other agencies need to become involved. Often, but not always, the practitioner's professional judgement will suggest a particular course of action, usually a referral to one or more additional services available locally. This process commonly requires the completion of a referral form, involving some information generic to all such processes – name, date of birth, number of siblings – and some that is specific to the agency being referred to. It is good practice in such cases to discuss the referral with the child's family and obtain their views of the situation. For some families, this is a process they will have to repeat several times as different agencies become involved.

This experience of repeating the same information and telling the same story several times to different practitioners was one of the reasons behind the introduction of the Common Assessment Framework (CAF). As its name suggests, the intention is that staff in all situations use the same process for referral on to, and between, other agencies. While, in many instances, the additional support the child or young person requires is seemingly obvious, the use of the CAF is intended to ensure that a holistic view is taken and that all avenues are addressed, so that it is clear why the particular referral has been made, and what other avenues are, or are not, appropriate.

With its origins in the Department of Health's triangular assessment process, which considers child development, family and environment, the CAF is framed under a number of headings. For instance, in the child development area is 'emotional and social development'. Each area is then provided with a number of prompts, in this case including 'feeling special; early attachments; risking/actual self-harm; phobias; psychological difficulties; coping with stress; motivation; positive attitudes; confidence; relationships with peers; feeling isolated and solitary; fears; often unhappy'.[3] While it can be argued that no single professional will have all the knowledge of a child or young person necessary to make judgements fairly and to comment in all these areas, the process is not intended to represent solely the evidence and opinions of one individual. It is intended that others contribute to the process too.

A strong, underlying principle is that the child and their parents are involved, to the extent that not only are their comments recorded, but also their signatures to show that they understand the purposes for which the information will be used, and the degree to which it can be shared. They have the right to specify who can, and crucially who cannot, see it. In most instances the parent or carer will provide consent, but if this is not felt to be appropriate then the young person may, under the auspices of 'Gillick competence', give it themselves.[4]

As well as involving young people and their families in the CAF process, the involvement of a number of agencies should provide a breadth of information. However, if a child or young person has more than one professional involved with them, it is possible that they are beyond the remit of the CAF process, which is intended to help determine what actions, and what services, are necessary to support them effectively. The CAF has been introduced for referrals that have yet to meet a statutory level; in the case of child protection procedures, for instance, the process would not be followed, as an intensive investigation and intervention would already have been triggered (although an initial CAF assessment may expose sufficient concerns to trigger such a procedure, subsequently making this process redundant).

The CAF process raises a number of issues: when should one be completed? who should take the main responsibility for it? how do you know whether someone else has already begun to do one? what denotes 'completion'? In part, these are addressed by the flags system of ContactPoint, where completion of a CAF can be signalled to others. Also, because of the intention that all agencies should contribute to the referral, it is likely, although not guaranteed, that initial enquiries will reveal who else is involved with the child or young person. However, not every instance will require that all boxes are filled in, and sometimes information may be difficult to acquire, with the possibility of intervention being delayed while enquiries are made. Ultimately it will be professional judgement, and the child's and family's consent, that determine when any particular round of the CAF completion process can be thought to be over.

Once completed, a signed, printed copy of the CAF is deposited in a central repository in each local authority. In many instances, these will also be stored electronically so that the contents can be shared more easily between those involved with the child or young person, or subsequently allocated to them.

However, it is not just the creation of the document that is important, but the process of holistic assessment and the services that this may provide access to. Although the intention is that the process of completion should help bring a focus to bear on what actions to take, in many instances this will have been decided before the CAF was begun. This may raise the question: why complete the CAF if the referral has already been decided? One reason is to provide for the receiving services a view of the child and their situation that is as rounded as possible. Another is to ensure all aspects really have been considered, and therefore confirm that the requested service is the correct one. There is also a move to have all paperwork become 'CAF-compliant', following the format of the CAF, so that some uniformity is achieved and, should an onward referral prove necessary, the work has already begun.

In instances where the next step for support for the child is not clear, the CAF will be taken to a multi-agency forum such as a Social Inclusion Panel, for consideration and to determine the next course of action. Typically, such a group will be made up of members of children's social care, the youth offending team, child and adolescent mental health, education social workers, out-of-school provisions such as the Pupil Referral Unit, youth service, and voluntary sector representatives for support that has been commissioned from the third sector. It is possible that representatives of mainstream schools will also attend, as these are the biggest single provider of services to young people.

If the CAF is in electronic format, members may have looked at it in advance, or may receive it electronically at the meeting or share it on a large-screen display such as an interactive whiteboard. However, it is still most likely that paper copies will be handed around and, following a scan of the contents, the most appropriate agency or multiples thereof allocated to step in.

It is usually at this point that the role of lead professional will be determined. This is a key worker who coordinates the input of all others and acts as the primary contact for the child or young person and their family. It may well be that the person who completed the CAF is asked to take this on, as they possibly know the situation better than the others, although this need not be the case.

In order to ensure that everyone, whether a referring agency or a family, is aware of the full range of available support, all local authorities are required to develop an online Children's Services Directory. This is a searchable resource of all local providers that lists the support they are able to offer, along with contact details.

Once the range of necessary inputs has been determined, and allocation of the lead role decided, the various agencies can begin to work together. Clearly one issue, despite the allocation of a coordinating role, will be ensuring that each knows what the other is doing. While meetings can help to agree objectives and keep updated, ICT has an important function here.

Joined-up working

In the first instance, the technology allows the concerns of the CAF to be shared easily. Secondly, email provides a simple way to keep each professional informed of any actions and concerns. However, each service involved will have its own recording system, so some actions may not be noted centrally. One solution is to have a shared, online case-management system, in which all activity is logged and a joint chronology built up from collective records.

Such an approach to case management is one development made possible by putting the CAF process online. If the form itself can be shared, and contributions made by staff working in different locations, then when follow-up actions are taken these can be related to the initial concerns that were raised.

One example of this is part of the ShareCare suite of software developed by Esprit.[5] Once the electronic CAF, or e-CAF, has been completed and the appropriate course of action determined, this system can be used for case management and monitoring. By linking in the electronic children's services directory a multi-disciplinary team can be allocated to the case. They can be notified of the allocation by email, which will also notify them automatically of any updates to the files, or of meetings and case conferences that are called.

Each team member can contribute to a shared chronology of actions and events, and they can jointly undertake further assessments and evaluations of outcomes, and contribute to decision-making, such as closing the intervention if it is successful, or referring on to other agencies if not.

Deciding who should do what

Behind such a system sit a number of safeguards. These include having in place information-sharing agreements between all agencies involved. Typically, this will be between children's services (representing children's social care and education services, including schools), the health authority, in the form of both the primary care trust and child and adolescent mental health, and the police. Where members of the voluntary sector are commissioned to provide services, they too may be signatories. This does not mean, though, that all signatories can access information in the same way. The police, for instance, may well contribute information to raise concerns about a child or young person, but may not have access to information from other agencies, partly because such access may compromise future investigations.

Having agreed to share information, these agencies will determine and implement a 'permissions matrix', a mechanism that determines which staff, at what level, have access to which elements of a child's online file. Staff in voluntary agencies, for instance, may have very restricted access, as they may be part-time volunteers with little or no training and weak supervision and accountability mechanisms. In that case, it may not be feasible to impose on them the same level of expectations of professional behaviour as for those with a level of qualification in a particular field.

That is not to say that all qualified professionals will have unfettered access to all information on every child. Medical information, for instance, may be restricted to medical staff, even though concerns about school achievement or general socialisation are shared more freely.

Such protocols are intended to provide safeguards to confidential information so that records become available only to practitioners who are involved with a particular child and, despite the intentions of making information-sharing easier, such access is restricted to the information that is appropriate to the role of each of them. This may vary between the lead professional, who will coordinate all others, their line manager, and practitioners providing particular services, such as weekend respite care.

The permissions matrix also enacts the aspect of the CAF that gives the right to parents and young people to determine who may, and may not, view its contents. Not just agencies, but specific roles and individuals within them, can be disbarred from access. While this may seem to run the risk of putting personalities before practice, it can also initiate conversations about, and consideration of, the different roles and expectations of those fulfilling them – both positively and negatively.

Case study – How ICT enhances completion of the CAF

Although involved in the development of a fully functioning e-CAF with a case-management and referral system built in, staff in Tower Hamlets in east London created an electronic form to pre-empt the longer-term introduction of a fully online system, and to enable a somewhat modified and enhanced approach to the initial assessment. The form[6] uses the headings of the existing CAF, and through the use of macros in Excel builds in some other supporting features.

The enhancements are intended to support an assessment that has elements of a solution-focused approach.[7] To this end, the form uses pop-up boxes that suggest 'risk' and 'protective' factors, in order to help identify both concerns, and the resources the child and the family have that may help mitigate these. For instance, the former will be aspects of the situation that are inhibiting the child's development towards one of the key outcomes. The latter will be those that work in some way to alleviate the situation, or that can be drawn on to support change. They represent the ends of a continuum. Under the heading 'Family history, functioning and well-being', for example, the protective factor is 'The child's family is adaptable and easily accommodates the needs of the child', whereas the risk factor is 'The child's family is inflexible and the needs of the adults are consistently to the fore'.

There is then a similar pop-up to help with completion of the 'Evidence' box, where guidance from the Department for Children, Schools and Families is made available, along with any local additions for the practitioner to show how they came to their conclusion. This box is deliberately limited in size to take no more than 1000 characters, so that evidence has to be concise, but also so that they may have to give their attention to other areas of the form in order to get their observations down. For the same aspect, 'Family history, functioning and well-being', the suggested evidence includes:

Culture, size and composition of the household – including changes in the people living in the accommodation since the child's birth

Family history – including any concerns about inheriting illnesses from a parent

Family routines

Disorganised/chaotic lifestyle

Failure to show care or interest in the baby, child or young person

Impact of problems experienced by other family members, such as physical illness, mental health problems, bereavement or loss

Allowing the baby, child or young person to witness violent behaviour, including domestic violence (both physical and verbal)

Involvement in criminal activity/anti-social behaviour

Experience of abuse

Family relationships – including all people important to the baby, child or young person, e.g. the impact of siblings, absent parents and any serious difficulties in the parents' relationship

History of family breakdown or other disruptive events

Parental physical and mental health (including depression) or disability

Involvement in alcohol misuse
Involvement in substance abuse/misuse
Family's attitude to tobacco/child is exposed to passive smoking
Whether anyone in the family presents a risk to the child.

There is then an opportunity to record a score between one and five – one being that this element of the assessment is one that does not raise concerns, and five being that this is an area of real worry, based on where the child is on the continuum given the evidence. These scores are then accumulated on a summary page. The intention is not to suggest that there is a numerical trigger point for intervention (it is not totalled), but rather to give a quick, visual picture of where the areas of greatest need are within the triangular assessment, and also where the existing strengths and resources lie that may be drawn upon to help resolve and alleviate whatever issues need to be addressed. Scaling also provides a useful tool for monitoring and review.

The nature of the CAF is for the subject and their family to be involved in its completion, so they will contribute to determining where they currently are on the one to five scale. In the solution-focused approach, determining where someone is on a scale provides a starting point; the next question is what one point higher up the scale would look like. This focuses on small, incremental steps rather than on an instant resolution.

At the point of review, these areas can be revisited and rescored to give a picture of the current situation and, by comparing the scores, of any movement that has occurred. In this way the efficacy, or otherwise, of any intervention can be discussed, or reasons for changes considered. As a number of reviews take place, so the changing situation over time can be seen, giving deeper insight into both the areas of concern and the ways sought to alleviate them.

ICT to raise alerts before problems arise

There are several ways in which ICTs are being used to help us identify children and young people who are at risk in some way, or who could be considered vulnerable. Some are used for observation and identification, others for monitoring and tracking. All of them raise moral and ethical issues, and questions about the role of technology when deployed to these ends. However, such uses do not mean removing the human factor from making critical judgements, nor absolving them from responsibility, particularly in dealing with the moral and ethical issues surrounding such uses, as the technology itself is morally neutral.

In the first instance, there is the very immediate method of monitoring children and young people offered by the use of CCTV, not only in public spaces but also in classrooms. Use of these systems means that misdemeanours can be spotted as they occur, or miscreants found after the event by running the tape back. While there is an argument to suggest that in some areas of the school this will help to achieve the outcome of 'staying safe', the use in classrooms is less well defined. A number of reasons have been given for why such systems have been installed, although generally it is either for monitoring of pupil behaviour in class, or for observation of staff, purportedly for professional development reasons.

The use of CCTV to monitor a classroom is little different from its use in a shopping centre or on a street corner, except that in this instance there is likely to be an adult in the room charged with ensuring that behaviour is acceptable. In order to ensure this is the case, a number of strategies will be in use, most designed to generate a positive, supportive, mutually respectful ethos – not just policing pupils and catching them misbehaving.

The argument for surveillance of staff in classrooms is based on one of professional development – it is an extension of the observation structure employed as part of performance-management procedures, only less obtrusive than having a line manager sitting at the back of the class. This also means that such observation can take place at any time without prior arrangement or the agreement of the teacher concerned.

> Such use of this technology needs to be weighed against the provision for safety and security. On the other hand, in most other parts of the school, the pupils' right to privacy (as well as that of teachers and other school workers), and the essential freedom of teaching, weigh against the need for permanent CCTV surveillance. This is so particularly in classrooms, where video surveillance can interfere not only with students' freedom of learning and of speech, but also with the freedom of teaching. The same applies to leisure areas, gymnasiums and dressing rooms, where surveillance can interfere with rights to privacy.
>
> These remarks are also based on the right to the development of the personality, which all children have. Indeed, their developing conception of their own freedom can become compromised if they assume from an early age that it is normal to be monitored by CCTV. This is all the more true if webcams or similar devices are used for distance monitoring of children during school time.
>
> (EC, 2008)

There are few instances to date of CCTV being adopted as standard equipment in British classrooms, despite the technology being available for some years, and a seeming acceptance that such surveillance is desirable for general protection.

However, there may be more willingness in schools to use ICT for surveillance purposes in other ways. Policy Central, for instance, is a system from Forensic Software[8] that monitors use of the school computer network and raises alerts when possible breaches of the acceptable-use policy arise. It works by constantly monitoring language in any open application, and being sensitive to key words – taken from different lists built around themes such as drugs or online grooming. If any words or phrases from these lists occur, the program grabs a screenshot and sends an email to designated responsible members of staff to review and decide on a course of action. For instance, a pupil sending an abusive email threatening to beat up a classmate would have the evidence instantly captured, and any situations arising from it would be nipped in the bud immediately.

Configuration possibilities within the system allow weightings of seriousness to be loaded against words, or require a number of repetitions, which together trigger the alert and indicate its priority nature. Lists can be switched on and off, and individual words allowed or added to the list of those causing action, so classwork in PSHE, for instance, on the theme of 'drug abuse' could see a temporary relaxation of that particular list for a specific class during the period of study.

While the automatic nature of such a system offers perceived protection for pupils (as victims, but also for early intervention for possible perpetrators) and detection of adults misusing the network, it also raises issues about continuous surveillance of everyone in the school community. Schools have always had a policing function for the young people in their care, but the notion of constantly monitoring activity for possible breaches, and checking every instance thereof, suggests that all users should be considered as likely as each other to act other than in accordance with school policies. In reality, there are likely to be few instances of anyone straying beyond the boundaries of what is acceptable, and in most institutions none of the more extreme criminal activity to which the internet lends itself. Before employing such systems, schools need to balance the existing structures – including promotion of positive, acceptable, behaviours – against the messages inherent in the deployment of these technological possibilities and a realistic assessment of the need for them.

Such systems can also change relationships in a school, from one where everyone is encouraged to be responsible and to act accordingly, to one where the message is that everyone is under suspicion, so constant policing is necessary. The use, or not, of such systems may support the intention of ensuring every child stays safe, but may also be seen as a method that focuses on the negative, rather than on proactive actions such as nurturing positive, trusting relationships where pupils feel that issues that arise, such as online bullying, can be brought to the attention of staff and feel confident that they will be dealt with accordingly.

Using ICT to help identify those in need of support

Monitoring a school network is not the only way in which ICT can be used to raise alarms and bring a child or young person to the attention of a responsible adult. One approach, developed by Esprit (see above), is the RYOGENS system.

Originally funded by the Office of the Deputy Prime Minister, this is a system intended to identify young people at risk of becoming involved in offending prior to them committing an offence, and providing diversionary interventions to prevent that happening. This aim is reflected in the acronym RYOGENS: Reducing Youth Offending Generic Electronic National Solution.

The approach originated out of the Youth Inclusion and Support Panel part of the youth justice arrangements in each authority. This group uses an assessment known as ONSET, which lists a number of factors that suggest whether a young person is likely to become involved in crime. RYOGENS took these factors, distilled them to a list of 40, then put them online so that when a child or young person comes to the attention of a service, any concerns that match these can be shared through the system. If sufficient concerns are raised, the system automatically sends a message to an administrator, who will assess the situation and determine what action, if any, to take, then notify the appropriate service. The indicators include:

- missed medical appointment
- self-harm
- child/substance misuse
- parent/substance misuse
- social isolation.

The various factors can be weighted so a numerical trigger point is reached that sends out an alert. 'Self-harm' will be sufficient in its own right to warrant further investigation, whereas 'social isolation' may not. It is clear that many young people could meet such criteria while never becoming involved in criminal behaviour, yet if they were subject to a number of such indicators, there is clearly cause for concern and a likely need for support.

While the system was developed to direct attention to children and young people at risk of offending, it is clear that many of the factors indicating this are also factors that indicate vulnerability to many other risks.

The RYOGENS system is also capable of receiving data from other sources, so where children and young people may be known to a number of agencies, it can be used as a way of bringing together information that otherwise may not be connected, again leading to the possibility of an escalation of concern and intervention due to its amalgamation.

Should an alert lead to an intervention, the system then enables the practitioners involved to share case-management facilities. This includes logging their activities, and uploading pertinent files such as case reports or review notes for others to see; also for the referral to be sent back should an intervention prove ineffective or further action be required.

While the imprecision of the concerns has been one criticism of the system, another has been that concerns can be logged without the permission of the subject or their family. There is a check box to say that permission has been sought, which has to be ticked before completion of the process of recording a concern. However, there is also the facility to create the record without this being the case, which is facilitated by the inclusion of a list of reasons why the particular issues can be raised and recorded without such agreement. Users can check another box stating that permission was not sought, then give up to three reasons to show why, within a legal framework, this was the case. These caveats are each drawn from a number of acts, including 'Taking reasonable steps to identify children in need' (Children's Act 1989, part 1 of schedule 2, para. 1, Applies to LAs and professionals in other sectors).

While use of RYOGENS has diminished across the authorities where it was piloted, many of its developments can be seen in the subsequent ShareCare packages, with their hierarchies for information-sharing, their case-management tools, and the ability to upload relevant documentation. Whilst this system sought to enable information-sharing among practitioners to enable early intervention, with legal guidance to support this process, once a child is identified as needing support the CAF assessment starts, and the involvement of families and young people is required in determining how the information is shared.

ICT to support 'enjoying and achieving'

The analysis of data to monitor pupils' progress is becoming increasingly sophisticated. Whereas school reports once gave grades and levels based on internal hierarchies and impressions, the introduction of the National Curriculum has meant that norm referencing is used to give an assessment that should be uniform across the country. And within the levels there are sub-levels, so that even small steps of progress can be recognised. This is particularly true since the introduction of the P levels (pre-National Curriculum), brought in to measure the progress of pupils whose achievement is not expected to exceed level two of the National Curriculum throughout their school career.

Many schools have bespoke systems, often built on Excel spreadsheets, to perform the tracking function, although there is also now a national database system for all schools, and Ofsted, to use to perform this function.

As discussed in previous chapters, the Department for Education and Skills provided the Pupil Achievement Tracker (PAT) and the Performance and Achievement (PANDA) report to provide data tracking for schools. These gave information on individual pupils and aggregated figures, and made comparisons with statistically similar schools across the country. (These 'statistical neighbours' might include schools with similar profiles for the numbers of pupils from ethnic minorities, or numbers of pupils eligible for free school meals, or with pupils from areas of multiple deprivation.)

In 2007 the PAT and PANDA were combined to create a more powerful system that could deal with data from the level of an individual pupil, through to the whole school, and beyond this to the complete local authority. In between these extremes it can be filtered by particular cohorts such as year, gender, ethnicity and special educational needs, and analysed by factors known as 'contextual value-added' (see Chapter Four for a breakdown of the factors). Contextual value-added takes variables that are known to affect pupils' performance and applies them to the data to give an overall rating of how effective the school is, given the circumstances it is in and the challenges it faces. Under this system, a score of 100 is average, so a score above this norm suggests that a school is performing better than can be expected given the circumstances within which it is working. The intention of such a process is to provide a levelling effect, so schools in affluent areas, with aspirational intakes, can be challenged to raise their pupils' performance in the same way that those in deprived inner-city areas can be. These contextual value-added factors take into account factors such as gender, as well as less well recognised factors that affect performance, such as the point at which a child was born in the school year, and pupil mobility.

With this system, the intention is to be able to interrogate the data through greater levels of granularity: from the level of whole-school performance down to any individual, and beyond that to their answers to any question in a particular SAT assessment. RAISEonline provides the analysis with which Ofsted starts its inspections, although schools can download a 'mirror' version of their data and add additional information to provide a richer, more meaningful assessment of their performance. By placing pupil results in a context of stability, welfare and aspiration, it has become possible for Ofsted to make more considered, nuanced judgements which suggest that even seemingly high-performing schools could stretch their pupils further, while those in areas of inner-city deprivation are doing a very good job, despite the circumstances their pupils find themselves in.

The ability of the system to aggregate results also gives local authorities a means of assessing performance across their whole area. Again, this can be analysed in different ways, but could include attainment of pupils with special educational needs or of those in a particular ward or wards, or pupils from designated ethnic groups. By interrogating the data to this degree, decisions can be made about resource allocation across the authority, and about targeting interventions to particular groups or localities.

RAISEonline is not the only data analysis tool that schools use. Since 2000, the Fischer Family Trust[9] has been supporting schools by providing sets of data to support analyses of school performance and future target-setting. Many of the variables included are similar to those found in RAISEonline. However, the data cover a broader range of subjects, so schools can interrogate them for the full range of subjects and courses available at Key Stage 4, for instance.

Another source of information that schools use in order to track possible achievement outcomes for pupils are the Cognitive Abilities Tests (see also Chapter One), which are often taken in year seven as pupils enter secondary schools, and can be repeated in year ten. These measure such aspects as verbal reasoning in order to predict future progress, alongside other factors such as SATs results in years six and nine.

Reaching further in school and beyond

Using the wider connectivity available through the internet can also support the goal of children and young people enjoying and achieving by expanding the boundaries of learning in all its aspects – when, where and how it can happen.

One of the goals of Harnessing Technology is that by spring 2008 every pupil should have access to a 'personalised online learning space' (DfES, 2005a), a so-called 'learning platform'. Secondary schools, in particular, are being encouraged to invest in these, especially those involved in the Building Schools for the Future programme, where the provision of learning platforms is part of the mandatory requirements. While there is some debate around a precise definition of exactly what one might be, Becta has provided guidance about functionality and activities.

A learning platform brings together hardware, software and supporting services to enable more effective ways of working. Learning platforms vary considerably, but every learning platform should provide a range of ICT-based functions including:

- Content management: enabling teaching staff to create, store and repurpose resources and coursework which can be accessed online
- Curriculum mapping and planning: providing tools and storage to support assessment for learning, personalisation, lesson planning, etc.
- Learner engagement and administration: enabling access to pupil information, attendance data, timetabling, e-portfolios and management information
- Tools and services: providing communication tools such as email, messaging, discussion forums and blogs.

Learning platforms enable:

- schools to provide education for pupils away from school: in hospital or pupil referral units, or at home (e.g. following exclusion from school)
- collaboration and sharing of resources between institutions
- common access to continuing professional development resources and courses
- rationalisation of training and support within a local authority or regional broadband consortium
- pupils to continue to access the same resources when they transfer between institutions.

(From 'What is a learning platform?' at
http://localauthorities.becta.org.uk)

Having set out what one is, Becta also provides a technical specification against which a number of products bearing the label were assessed in late 2006. Of those submitted (involvement was not compulsory), ten were found to meet the specification and were added to a list of Becta approved suppliers.[10] However, there are issues associated with this list, which is considered to be somewhat restricted. One very popular provision, which has all the functions but fails to meet the requirements, is not included. Moodle is an open source (licence-free) package that is very widely used in higher and further education and also in schools, yet it is not on the list because there is no single provider to take responsibility for supporting and developing it. Despite this, its popularity continues to grow. A survey by the British Educational Suppliers Association found that 'it is the most popular platform in secondary schools' (*Guardian Education Supplement*, 4 December 2007). While Becta is offering support to schools to procure a learning platform that is fit for purpose by following a set of clear, considered guidelines, it seems there is a degree of independence being demonstrated in putting this into action.

Regardless of the provider, there are a number of things that a learning platform should enable learners to be able to do. These might include:

- download learning materials, both in lessons and away from school – including text, images, video, audio and web-based resources such as podcasts
- communicate with teachers and classmates to discuss work; collaborate on tasks; receive help; critique work
- receive and submit work – including coursework and homework
- send in work for marking and receive feedback
- access materials from other schools – particularly when following courses at more than one institution
- view resources that have been uploaded from a central service or other schools
- store electronic materials such as work samples and coursework submissions
- take assessments online
- learn from remote sites through technology such as video-conferencing.

In addition to this provision for learning through the connectivity that the internet brings, there is also an aim that by 2010 learning platforms will be linked to school management information systems. This will allow for electronic or online marking to automatically synchronise with pupils' records. All teacher marking, assessment and recording of achievement can be recorded, and accessed not just by staff, but also by parents, at any time, rather than having to wait for the end-of-term report. Given that the role of the parent is seen as crucial to the attainment of pupils – their aspirations, attitudes towards education, and support for the school – such access should provide a means by which they can work in conjunction with teaching staff more easily.

However, there will be a need to provide information in a format that parents will understand, rather than in esoteric 'education-speak', and to find a shared vocabulary that facilitates that involvement.

Previously the degree to which schools have welcomed parents and carers as partners in the education of their children has varied considerably, with stories, possibly apocryphal, of lines drawn across playgrounds beyond which parents were not welcome without an appointment. Opening up pupil records will mean a more immediate appreciation of individual performance, which should lead in turn to a quicker response to difficulties, rather than waiting for the end-of-term report or the parents' evening. On the other hand, it may lead to parents regularly tracking progress and engaging teachers in dialogues that are not necessarily beneficial to the child's learning. Schools will no doubt be sensitive to the degree of information provided, and the extent to which correspondence with parents will be invited, although many teachers will welcome the opportunity to involve parents more easily in their offspring's performance.

Case study – Practise changing through implementation of a learning platform

Crossways Academy is a sixth form centre in Lewisham that opened in 2004 following the amalgamation of three local school sixth forms. It is already using ICT in many ways and is enhancing this under the Building Schools for the Future programme. Every student has access to a computer in lessons, and all resources are provided electronically through the learning platform as part of the managed service. These materials are also available when students log in elsewhere. For those who don't have a computer at home, the school can help families to buy them or provide short-term loans, and where necessary they will refund broadband subscriptions for time spent in online learning at home. As well as desktops and laptops, every room has an interactive whiteboard, and some are equipped with visualisers. The drama studio has facilities for recording, both sound and vision, and there are plans to begin using PDAs.

Before the school first opened, staff had time to populate the learning platform with lesson materials, making it easier for them to get started when the students arrived. This is reinforced with weekly opportunities for professional development, and ongoing support is given, with continuing to develop the online learning resources.

The school uses its management information system to track progress and keep parents informed of how their children are getting on. Homework can be handed in online and completion recorded by the teacher. In some instances, when pupils fall behind with homework, their swipe card is blocked so when they try to get into school on the Monday morning they find they can't. They are then directed to the head teacher's office to give an account of why they haven't completed their work, before the card is reactivated.

Because records are constantly updated, the school provides reports online to parents four times a year, rather than just one at the end of the year, and there are plans to move to providing access for parents at any time so they will have the same information as teachers. Eventually, more information about attainment and progress and attendance records will also be immediately available.

Much activity at the school is recognisably traditional, in subject choice and delivery through lessons in a structured timetable. However, it is also demonstrating how new technologies can enhance existing practice and begin to ease barriers between learning, in school and out.

However, as possibilities broaden for lesson delivery at Crossways and schools like it, there may be a need to define a new paradigm for attendance. Currently, state schools offer 380 sessions per year at which a pupil should be present – 39 teaching weeks (190 days) split into morning and afternoon. If pupils are able to access learning materials from any place at a time of their choosing, requisites of time and space no longer hold good – it seems that current notions of attendance, and absence, will need to be reconstructed.

The development of online feedback and recording of assessment, along with the prospect of pupils learning at times, and in places, that suit them, offers the possibility of greater pupil involvement in, and responsibility for, their own learning – a key aspect of personalisation. They can become less the recipients of teachers' analyses of their performance, and more the narrators of the story of the construction of their skills and knowledge. Allowing students to determine, at least in part, when and where learning happens also shifts the balance from attending to learn, to attending to learning. That is, instead of turning up at a certain time and place to receive an education, they will themselves ensure that learning takes place, and where and when.

Reaching out to teach the difficult-to-reach

The ability to reach out to children and young people who are beyond the accepted boundaries of time and space in the traditional model of schooling also offers the opportunity to engage with those who have become largely disengaged from the education system, and even from society as a whole – those considered 'socially excluded'. Within this broad category there are a number of identifiable groups, along with those who are less easily categorised but who have become disaffected for some reason. There are also those who could be placed under one of these labels, but who would not consider themselves as being on the margins of society.

The ranks of the socially excluded children and young people might include:

- teenage mothers
- asylum-seekers and refugees, including those who arrive unaccompanied
- those with a disability, including learning difficulties
- the chronically ill, including those with mental health problems
- the young homeless
- those who are leaving institutions, including children's homes or foster care
- gypsies and travellers, including families that tour with fairs and circuses
- young people with low basic skills, particularly when looking to work and become economically independent
- young people of post-compulsory education age who are not in employment, education or training
- those who are out of school for a sustained period, either voluntarily, due to school phobia for instance, or involuntarily because of exclusion.

Clearly, belonging to one or more of these groups does not automatically mean that the child or young person is socially excluded, nor does the absence of any such label mean that they are not. The term is not precisely defined, although it may be evident by the degree of engagement, or lack thereof, with universal services, in this context particularly education. ICT can offer those who are on the periphery of society support in a number of ways that can help move them towards the Every Child Matters outcomes.

One way, as previously mentioned, is to provide education at a distance for those who find it difficult to engage fully with schools or colleges, and so can't, or won't, physically attend. With the development of learning platforms, schools can post learning resources for students to access, provide correspondence with teachers and peers to facilitate working, and give feedback and assessments on work submitted. However, those who are disengaged physically can find it difficult to engage virtually, so may not use the opportunities offered.

There are a number of companies that provide online learning for those who are difficult to reach, such as Accipio Learning and Nisai Virtual Academy.[11] The latter offers a number of subjects: for Key Stage 2 (upper primary), the choice is limited to literacy and numeracy, expanding to these an additional seven others in Key Stage 3, which are then offered at GCSE level in Key Stage 4. English Literature, Maths and ICT are then available at AS Level.

Despite these courses being online, they are taught in real time and pupils are given a timetable of when to log on to attend lessons. Typically there will be four sessions in a day, each of about 45 minutes to an hour duration, when they are required to be present, along with an equal amount of time spent in follow-up work. All the lessons are recorded, so if one is missed it can be retrieved from the archive and caught up with later.

When working online, students are allocated to small groups, each logging on individually to a computer either at home or in a suitable location. On the monitor, the majority of space is given over to a working area where resources, including interactive materials, can be displayed. The teacher will talk over a headset to deliver the lesson, and can hand over control of the screen display for learners to get involved. Students have headsets too, although there is also a text messaging area which they often prefer to use rather than speaking aloud. The names of those present are listed on the left of the screen, so everyone knows who is attending the lesson that day, and linked to this are a number of icons so that pupils can communicate quickly. This might be virtually putting their hand up to ask, or answer, a question, or to show that they have finished working something out. After the lesson, they complete tasks to reinforce and demonstrate what they have learned, which are emailed to the tutor for marking and feedback.

The exam results for the Nisai Virtual Academy for the 2006–07 session are quite impressive, with 68 per cent of passes in the A–C range at GCSE, and 100 per cent of A Levels at A–C.

Case study – Re-engagement through online learning

Lizzie (a pseudonym) is a student at the Cherokee Project (Personalised Learning) of the Specialist Behaviour Service for Bath & North East Somerset. She is one of 35 students enrolled at a provision for those in the last two years of compulsory education who are becoming disengaged from mainstream education, to varying degrees, because of behaviour difficulties. Some are permanently excluded, others are placed part-time while also attending their parent school. All have a timetable of 25 hours per week, made up of a number of different elements including group work, outward bound courses, online courses, enrolment at a further education college, and work experience.

The online courses are modules from vision2learn from Creating Careers,[12] who specialise in providing vocational and pre-vocational courses delivered in this way. The courses followed at the Cherokee Project range from 'Finding my dream career' and 'Healthy eating and healthy living' to the iMedia qualification. About 20 of those attending the project in the academic year 2007–08 will have had an element of online learning in their timetable, while 13 of these will take this through to complete an accredited qualification.

Before being referred to the Cherokee Project, Lizzie had a very chequered school career, with several periods out of education that left her disillusioned and lacking in self-confidence. Working online suited her, as she could work at her own pace and was not distracted by other people unless she wanted to be. Below, she reflects on her experiences of online learning.

What courses have you taken online?

I have been working on the iMedia course plus Dream Job through vision2learn for schools. I have also been working to improve my ICT skills, literacy and numeracy on the computer. I should pass a couple of these this year, maybe more.

How is learning online different from learning in a classroom?

You don't have to do things at certain times, you can do it when you want. It's also sometimes harder if you don't understand something or are not sure of something, as there's no one around to ask. You can't mess around with your mates and get into trouble, but you can still see them after school, or at night, or on the weekends.

In what ways is it better?

I choose what I want to do and when. Yes, my keyworker tells me what I should meet for a target for the week, but they don't tell me when I have to do it. It's also better because I don't get into trouble. In school, I was always in trouble and my life really sucked, but since I was sent to Cherokee things have changed, a lot. I get treated as an adult and don't have to wear a uniform or put up with other students that I don't want to be around. My keyworker was even able to help me get a course at college because of the work I had done in the beginning, so I now have lots of opportunity to get a better job when I finish.

What have you been able to achieve online that you could not have done in school?

I have been able to complete work without getting into trouble. I should also get some qualifications which I wouldn't have been able to do because I was permanently excluded from two schools. I'm not in as much trouble at home any more and my Youth Offending Team worker doesn't need to see me any more.

Could anyone learn online?

I think most can learn, but whether they would want to or not, I don't know. If I don't do my work, my keyworker gets on my case, but she also praises me at our family meetings when I do complete the work. It helps me to keep going and not give up.

Should we do more learning online and less in classrooms?

Yes, if there's someone there to help you when you get stuck. Not right beside you all the time, but someone you can call, or a keyworker to help when they meet with you each week, something like that.

How could schools use online learning more effectively?

I think more qualifications need to be made for online learning at different levels, so people who can't do the work because it's too hard for them could do another level which isn't too hard. Then they could learn, and maybe do the next level at a different time. The courses also need to be shorter, maybe like a few weeks, so you don't get

> bored. I know a shorter course might not give you a qualification, but if there were a lot of them to choose from, and you needed a few of them to make a qualification, that would help.

Another approach

Despite its title, NotSchool.net is most certainly about education. It began in 2000 as a research project, then in 2007 became a charity to re-engage those who had become most disaffected from the education system – either having been rejected from it through exclusion, or disengaged from it for some other reason such as long-term sickness, school phobia or disillusionment. The title is a perhaps ironic statement that while this is education, it is not school. Its recent change of status has seen it change its name to the Inclusion Trust to reflect the broader objectives of not just providing education, but also having a wider interest in promoting social inclusion.

> The charity exists to advance learning opportunities for people that are excluded, or disengaged, from traditional education systems. In doing so we aim to make learning more accessible and engaging by harnessing new and emerging technologies and by supporting communities of learners within their own context and cultures.[13]

It is the intention to provide a paradigm of learning that is very different from that in the state education sector. Students become 'researchers', providers of learning materials are 'experts', and trained teachers who support small groups of no more than six participants are 'mentors'. Young people who join up are expected to be involved for at least six months, and to be completely out of the traditional education system. There is generally a roughly even gender balance, and most pupils are in the upper years of secondary school.

Researchers negotiate their own curriculum with their mentors, and it is reviewed at least every six weeks. This does not mean that core subjects such as numeracy, literacy and ICT are not covered – the core skills that these provide are recognised, but they may be delivered or reinforced through other topics, such as film-making or comedy.

Delivery is through FirstClass,[14] a well established online learning system widely used in universities, which provides a framework within which mentors and experts can post resources and researchers can respond, both in real time (through functions such as chat) and in their own time (using forums and message boards). There are also elements of the resource that allow for peer-to-peer communication and for collaboration on tasks.

Because of its virtual nature, researchers can participate and communicate at times that suit them. This has led to the recruitment of some mentors located abroad to meet the needs of participants who prefer to study when it is night time in the UK. There are also links to students overseas.

Where possible study is accredited, although not necessarily through traditional routes or with qualifications offered in schools, giving a creativity and flexibility that may not be possible in other settings. There are also internal certificates to validate learning.

Overall, the organisation has had some notable successes with the young people it has served.[15] However, the model is not one that suits all students. Some find it difficult to move beyond the norms of the more formal curriculum structure that they are used to, and that is still used by providers such as Nisai and Accipio. For many young people, it is the process of re-engagement, and the enfranchisement they are offered, that provide the success of NotSchool, bringing them back into learning and leading to further opportunities to enjoy and achieve in their lives.

Case study – Online learning as part of a continuum of provision

Ealing Federated Education Other Than At School (EOTAS) Service is not just one provision, but a whole range, providing a continuum of placements, different options for children and young people who are out of school. Some are provided by the local authority, such as the Pupil Referral Unit, others by the voluntary sector, and some by private concerns or charities. All suppliers of alternative education provision for the Ealing EOTAS Service continuum are on the Council's approved list, which ensures that commissioning of services is effective and that monitoring and quality assurance are undertaken according to clear performance indicators.[16] While all pupils are seen as potential candidates for returning to mainstream schools, some – particularly in the last years of compulsory education – will not, realistically, be able to make that step. The pupils the service works with may be referred for a number of reasons, including medical conditions, permanent exclusion, managed moves (where they are transferred between schools in a structured way in order to pre-empt possible permanent exclusion), and casual admissions (pupils who unexpectedly appear in the borough).

All are screened by one of two referral panels, one specifically for pupils in Key Stage 4, and decisions are then taken against predetermined criteria at the EOTAS Placement Panel regarding the most appropriate placement for them. Two of these options are online learning resources (Accipio Learning and NotSchool; see above). While both are designed and organised for working through the internet, they are sufficiently different in their structure and approach to attract different cohorts of pupils. In the academic year 2007–08, of the 210 pupils supported by the EOTAS service, 34 were placed with these two online learning organisations, 16 with Accipio and 18 with NotSchool, nearly all of whom were in

Key Stage 4 (the criteria for providing a pupil with a place with an online provision are very clear, and only with rare exceptions does this extend to younger pupils).

Accipio Learning was first used by the service in 2004, taking ten seats (the financial model is one of schools and authorities buying seats then allocating them to pupils, with the possibility of reallocating them during the year) – five for pupils at home and five working in a group. While the group was not particularly successful, the home use was, and led to an increase in places to 15 in the following year, at which level it has remained since. It was in 2006 that NotSchool was first used, as it was recognised that despite the range of provision, there were still some young people whose needs could be met more effectively through a somewhat different online service.

The criteria for seats with Accipio Learning are that pupils have difficulty working in an institutional environment, but have previously achieved reasonably well, in end of Key Stage 3 tests in particular. They also need to be capable of achieving between three and five GCSEs, and of having the motivation and commitment to work towards this. As well as academic ability, they also need to be able to work independently and to have sufficient basic skills – in literacy, numeracy and ICT – to be able to cope online without direct adult support. This isn't to say that, once pupils are allocated a place, the authority expects Accipio to take over completely. A teaching member of staff is allocated full time to support the programme, along with input from the Connexions Service and the authority's Social Inclusion Team (who work with schools to support pupils at risk of permanent exclusion). Having this degree of support means that pupils receive regular visits. Sessions are organised on Friday afternoons to extend the curriculum, and to ensure that pupils are not socially isolated. This is important because, despite the fact that all are from the same borough, they will not automatically be in the same class, and sometimes specific requests may have been made to keep them apart. Their classmates could be in any location around the country.

Pupils on this programme are also expected to have a moderate level of family support. This often builds on engagement with the system, and has led to parents not only sitting in on online lessons, but also seeking to improve their own skills by seeking out college courses.

The students at NotSchool have a similar profile, but are further along the continuum of provision. They have different and often quite complex needs, not necessarily educational ones. Not only will they have problems with working in an institutional environment, but they will also have high levels of disaffection, being quite distant from education, to the extent that they will have been unable to engage with other provisions within the EOTAS range. They will still need a level of skills in order to work independently, particularly with ICT and literacy, but they will also need something other than traditional, classroom-based learning. The support of at least one parent is also required in order for them to be considered for this resource.

While Accipio more closely follow the mode of learning found within schools – involving logging on according to a set timetable, receiving a taught, interactive lesson, and following it up with homework – it is recognised that some pupils find this a difficult model to engage with, whether in school or online. So some pupils that start with a seat at Accipio are then transferred on to NotSchool, although this is infrequent – no more than one or two per year.

Students who work with NotSchool have a different experience: not a completely unstructured one, but one in which they have a greater degree of control over the content of their curriculum. This is seen to some degree as a means of working with those who have difficulty in accepting authority, and in being organised and managed by adults as to what they will study. This isn't to say that there is no structure or control. Unlike Accipio, none of the engagement involves direct contact with a tutor, it is all online through the system in a similar way to email (Accipio uses voice and instant messaging), but if pupils transgress from accepted conduct they can have their connection turned off for a period, along with a communication about how they are expected to behave. Despite this seeming lack of structure, or overt focus on working towards recognised accredited outcomes, NotSchool has proved successful in re-engaging pupils in education who otherwise might have slipped into the category of not in education, employment or training, with all those leaving the provision in 2008 having a Post-16 Pathway identified. Indeed, 98 percent of them gain recognised, accredited, qualifications. In part, this is due to access to local staff, both a full-time worker supporting the scheme and a Connexions worker.

Students following courses with Accipio have more traditionally recognisable successes, although only at Foundation levels, as these are the only ones offered (the papers they sit are eligible for a C grade at best). Regardless of this limitation, pupils achieved exam success who otherwise may not have done so. One boy in 2007 passed Maths, English and double Science with C grades and ICT with a D, even though he spent part of year 11 in secure accommodation. Twelve students in that cohort achieved passes at some level. Recently, courses have been introduced to extend the range available, both basic skills which are at a lower academic level, and higher-level GCSEs which offer the possibility of top grades.

As well as the acknowledged, measurable successes offered by accreditation, there are a number of outcomes for individual pupils that are not as easy to quantify – stories of pupils gaining confidence and coping with otherwise difficult situations. One student who has a medical condition which makes her frequently faint now takes this in her stride, coming round and carrying on with her lessons. This was not the case previously. For another girl, the opportunity to construct a timetable for herself – one that she can dictate – brought an impasse to her challenging of authority. A boy on the periphery of trouble found that by working at home, he could avoid passing through environments that could make him susceptible to involvement in criminal activities.

Both ways of working online have provided learning opportunities for students that otherwise would not have been available. Many have achieved accredited academic success, and all have benefited by re-engaging with learning and not slipping beyond the reach of the available support. In part, this is has been to do with the resources themselves, although the strong local support and the belief in remaining in contact with pupils despite them learning online have clearly contributed considerably to this.

Smoothing upheaval

One possible use for online learning systems is for children and young people who are in public care – often referred to as 'looked-after children'. In this situation, they may find themselves moving between several different placements, and even to a variety of locations well away from their home authority. Wherever possible, local authorities, in their role as corporate parents, will try to minimise such disruption and find a suitable, stable placement as soon as possible. In this situation, a system that offers stable educational provision is to be welcomed. However, this may also mean that the student does not attend a local school at their placement, and so does not establish a group of friends or a social network in that area. The need for consistency in one aspect of their lives needs to be balanced with the broader needs of living and growing up in a different place.

It is also possible to offer some stability to learning by providing support through the internet from an established school, particularly if the placement is only short term, if a child's parent needs to be hospitalised, for instance. As the use of learning platforms develops, even in primary schools, so the potential for providing resources to pupils who are away from school, not just those in care, but also those who are ill or temporarily excluded, will grow. Staff will post lesson content, and students will complete it and submit it. Work can also be stored in the e-portfolio for access and transfer to new establishments.

However, the internet already offers a range of ways in which looked-after children are being supported, without the need for the formalised structure of a learning platform. Email allows teachers to send work and receive replies. Similarly, it can facilitate contact with social workers and family members.

Storage can also be provided through many of the virtual vaults included in packages from internet service providers.

There are also some services tailored specifically for looked-after children. The Who Cares? Trust[17] is dedicated to supporting them and provides online resources, at one time including the CareZone, a secure repository for electronic storage, although this is now closed. More recently, the Trust has developed an online magazine, *Who Cares? Xtra*, with content applicable to young people in care aged between 12 and 18. This includes information about rights, a problem page, and first-hand accounts of different situations, such as being in a secure unit. This helps promote a sense of belonging to a wider community – that while they may be the only looked-after child in a school, there are others with whom they can connect. This is reinforced by the use of a message board. Other organisations, such as the Adolescent and Children's Trust, are also building children's forum areas into their websites.[18]

One of the issues for looked-after children that arises from disruptions in their placements is that of belonging, and of having a fragmentary sense of personal history. By using online tools for learning, some continuity can be built up, along with online storage so that work is not lost in any upheaval. Alongside this, it can create a semblance of stability and community, connect them to people – peers, family and professionals – and go some way to reducing disturbance in young lives.

On the road

Another group who find themselves in different locations, although in this instance quite deliberately, and often in a planned and predictable way, are children from travelling families, including those whose families work in circuses and funfairs. These latter groups in particular have base schools in places where they spend the winter, but there is an inevitable disruption from April to October when they tour the country. Since the early 1980s, many have been provided with learning packs to cover this period. However, these have not always proved engaging, and using the postal service to send in work and get it back with teachers' comments has been a barrier to them being completed.

In order to address this problem, a project was started in 2003 to explore the use of ICT for distance learning. Initially 20 primary-age pupils were provided with laptops with data cards, which use the mobile phone network to connect to the internet. The E-Learning and Mobility Project (ELAMP) has gradually been expanding ever since; by the 2007 travelling season, around 400 school-age children from 39 local authorities were regularly using the equipment for learning, with more than 90 per cent of them thought to be making satisfactory or good progress.[19]

The project has developed in a number of ways since its inception. Initially it was aimed at primary-age pupils, but in 2005 it was decided to explore two new avenues: supporting pupils from ten secondary schools, and working with children from gypsy families.

It was anticipated that working with secondary schools would prove problematic due to the need to coordinate a number of subject teachers rather than just a single class teacher. Organising this group of teachers proved to be key to getting positive outcomes, and the project was sufficiently successful for funding to continue since then.

Working with gypsy children was thought to be challenging because of the less predictable movements of this group, as well as their being more circumspect in their commitment to traditional patterns of education. One way of dealing with this has been to leave laptops and web access with families throughout the year, not just when they are on the road.

In subsequent years, the ELAMP project has begun to focus on older children in travelling families, who may have become disengaged from education altogether, perhaps seeing it as irrelevant to their lifestyle, particularly as they are learning job skills from their families and are likely to continue to work in fairs and circuses. To address this, students in Key Stage 4 have been provided with a learning framework from Nisai (see above), with content developed by the charity Chrysalis – Club 2000,[20] which supports them in achieving qualifications based on wider key skills within the Award Scheme Development and Accreditation Network (ASDAN)[21] framework. Within the project, learners are known as 'members' and tutors as 'advisors'. They engage in projects such as 'Pricing a job' or 'Planning a party', for which they gather evidence of their capabilities in a range of formats and upload into a portfolio. There are encouraging initial results for take-up and engagement with this curriculum.

The steady growth of the ELAMP project and its gradual development to meet the needs of a wider constituency is a very practical demonstration of the possibilities of any time, any place, any where learning.

Conclusion

The objective of providing opportunities for children and young people to develop in every aspect of their lives, and to be enabled to achieve the five outcomes, is made easier through the use of ICT. It can help us to make connections – about them, for them, and with them – that otherwise would be difficult to make. Through these we can identify problems earlier and more easily, then complete broad-based, multi-agency assessments and provide timely interventions. Those allocated to provide this support to children and their families can do this better through communicating about what they are doing, monitoring progress beyond their own sphere of activity, and maintaining an up-to-date understanding of the situation and the ways in which concerns are being met.

At school, ICT can help staff to know pupils, their achievements and their potential more accurately. Teachers can take individuals' preferences into account when planning lessons, and students can work in ways that they know benefit them most, making it personal. This may include not attending school in the traditional sense. In some circumstances, for those who find schools difficult places to be, for whatever reason, online learning provides a way of accessing education without needing to enter a school. And for the education system, it offers a way of giving all children a chance to learn when other options are restricted. It brings closer to learning pupils who have moved beyond the reach of schools, so that even in challenging situations they continue to matter.

Chapter 4

A web for learning

The education system is beginning to transform, to respond to the changing needs of young people, and of the society in which they will find themselves living in the future. Ways of working, communicating and interacting are shifting, often with surprising speed. In order to lead to active citizens who can make a positive contribution, achieve economic wellbeing and continue to learn, the way in which schooling is provided also needs to change.

This chapter looks at the theoretical model underpinning these changes in schools – Personalised Learning. It considers what Personalised Learning is, and how it is reflected in the systems and structures in schools – not just technological ones, networks coming into place to provide a backbone for the delivery of such learning, but also evaluative ones, such as the role of Ofsted. It then discusses the new tools that technology is providing, which many learners are already using outside formal education, and the skills these help to develop – often the very ones asked for by the developing jobs market, that may be missing from the school curriculum.

Finally, there is an examination of some of the curriculum models coming into place to meet the new challenges in the education system, and the ways in which ICT is integral to these.

How will we know when learning is personalised?

There are five components to Personalised Learning, as outlined by the Department for Children, Schools and Families (DCSF).[1] They are split into two groups:

- the inner core – the element based on classroom practice –
  - Assessment for learning
  - Effective teaching and learning
  - Curriculum entitlement and choice
- personalising the school experience – elements that happen outside the classroom but support the personalisation process –
  - Organising the school
  - Beyond the classroom.

The latter two are seen as underpinning the whole endeavour.

> The inner core focuses on classroom practice. This is supported by a focus on arranging the school for Personalised Learning to set the pre-conditions for learning and remove the barriers to achievement. The use of ICT permeates all components as a way of enhancing creativity, extending learning opportunities and sustaining varied and challenging paces of learning through grouping arrangements. The components are an integrated whole and are mutually supportive. They offer a framework for implementation: a set of tools for schools and teachers to employ contextually so as to respond to the challenges they face.
>
> (www.standards.dfes.gov.uk/personalisedlearning/five)

These five components are not particularly revolutionary; they are the basis of much good, existing practice. **Assessment for learning** is essentially giving feedback to pupils to help them improve their outcomes and achievement. This is 'formative' rather than 'summative' assessment. The latter is the type of assessment typically encountered at the end of key stages – such as SATs tests and GCSEs – which gives a snapshot of the point at which a pupil has arrived at that particular time. Formative assessment examines work against the original learning objectives and offers guidance as to how it can be improved. This might happen with a piece of coursework, for instance, where a teacher ensures pupils' foci are on the desired outcomes and gives feedback that helps them to improve their work. In this instance there may eventually be a final assessment and a grade or mark given, but along the way teachers are more involved in providing guidance than in marking. Spread more widely over a pupil's school career, it involves tracking their progress and working with them to aim for the best possible outcomes for them.

When considering **Effective teaching and learning**, the intention is to ask teachers to draw on a diverse range of skills, to continue to develop these throughout their career, to make pupils aware of how the process of learning works, and to use this understanding to make this a productive process for themselves. The use of materials to focus on learning styles and multiple intelligences, along with approaches such as Accelerated Learning (discussed later in this chapter), are all supportive of this aspect of Personalised Learning.

One of the shifts represented in thinking about **Curriculum entitlement and choice** is that of focusing less on content, and more on skills and capabilities. This may give rise to a less prescriptive, subject-oriented timetable in secondary schools at least, with project-based work in the lower school, and diplomas with a range of routes and content for the post-14 age group. (Although there may also be a shift away from grouping pupils by age, with vertically grouped classes based on interest and achievement.) This shift in focus is reflected in innovative curriculum formats such as Enquiring Minds from Futurelab and Opening Minds from the Royal Society for the Encouragement of Arts, Manufactures and Commerce

(RSA) (both discussed later in this chapter). While this will not result in pupils completely choosing their own content, there should be more choices available for them, and more opportunities to take responsibility for their own learning.

A number of factors may influence **Organising the school**, many of them starting up in recent years. These include using the range of adults now found in schools to support pupils in different ways. These 'para-educators' include those focused directly on learning, such as teaching assistants, and also those whose jobs involve providing other support, such as learning mentors. The reform of the workforce is a reflection of the Every Child Matters agenda, aiming to support the child holistically in recognition of the impact that factors external to the school, and indeed to the child, can have on their ability to learn. Learning mentors, for instance, will support individual pupils, taking an interest in them and helping them deal with problems that might be getting in the way of them working effectively in lessons. Beyond this, there is a role for education social workers to deal with matters affecting attendance, usually linked to the home, although this may come under the remit of the home/ school liaison officer. Some schools, particularly under the Extended Schools umbrella (see Chapter One), may have social workers based within them, or make counsellors and therapists available for pupils. And it is not uncommon for secondary schools to have regular visits from school nurses, and to have police officers stationed with them as well.

Learning mentors may also contribute to whole-school initiatives to bring about behaviour for learning – an approach suggesting that appropriate ways of conducting oneself in school can be directly taught and learnt. Other elements that will have an impact on this include school design, where buildings, particularly new ones, are deliberately constructed to encourage acceptable behaviour – perhaps by removing bottlenecks, or areas where pupils can remain unseen, and introducing communal spaces where the whole school community can ensure people are respectful of the desired norms.

The elements of Personalised Learning that are contained in thinking about what a school offers **Beyond the classroom** are also those that seek to take a more holistic approach to children, offering them support to meet diverse needs. This involves knowing them more broadly than just in terms of school performance, and may need assistance from others, including social workers, Connexions advisors or community volunteers. Some of this involvement may happen outside lesson times, at breaks or in after-school clubs, and some may even be located away from school, in libraries or youth clubs. Some may also be supported by online tools, such as those employed for careers advice by Connexions.

Case study – Club Tech – out-of-school learning that complements the curriculum

Originally developed in the USA, Club Tech[2] is a collaboration between Microsoft and the Boys and Girls Clubs of America. Over the five years of the project since it began in 2002, over 2700 clubs across the USA have been equipped with hardware and software, and given training in the skills necessary to use it. An interactive training resource is provided for children to work through at their own pace, which also means that staff in each of the venues don't have to have ICT skills themselves in order to host a club.

Beyond basic computer skills, the initiative has also seen the development of a digital arts suite of programs to boost creativity. In order to promote them and to provide an incentive and real purpose, there is an annual festival to promote their use, with entries coming from across all the clubs in the country.

Having enjoyed success in the USA, this model is now being imported into the UK, although with some modifications, in a project led by Lisbeth Goodman of SMARTlab, based at the University of East London in Newham. Having recently completed a quality assurance review of the American set-up for Microsoft, she knows the workings of the project well. She was encouraged initially by the attitude of the funders. 'Microsoft are genuinely interested in building, from the ground up, community projects for kids,' she says, and when she approached the users she found a similar view. 'Having interviewed thousands of kids, parents, and volunteers the response was predominantly positive.'

Each location has a standard set-up, which includes the on-screen tutorial on basic user skills. This is important because, as Lisbeth points out, 'Quality and consistency are difficult to assure if you just donate the kit,' particularly in situations where the staff may be volunteers, and certainly not people recruited for their computer skills. 'You need a core curriculum, that kids can then leave,' she believes.

This is one area where there may be a difference in the way clubs are set up and resourced on this side of the Atlantic compared with the USA. These initial skills are less of an issue in this country, due to the place of ICT as a core curriculum subject in schools. It is an aspect that Lisbeth sees as key, particularly as she wants this project in the UK to provide a model that can be exported to other parts of Europe, then beyond into Africa and Asia. Scoping how this might work is part of the remit of two researchers who have been recruited to the project. Already the core skills units are being translated into 100 different languages and dialects in preparation for the project's further growth, and thought is being given to how these might need to be adapted for those with special needs.

Once club members have mastered the basic skills modules, they move on to the digital arts suite, a set of programs to encourage creativity, from which the opportunity arises to enter the annual Digital Arts event. While competition is not one of the core values of the project, this has been very successful in the USA, probably, at least in part, because college scholarships are on offer as prizes. For young people from the poorest neighbourhoods, these are very real incentives to enter and win.

It isn't just children who have benefited from the clubs. Those who were the most successful included instances of wider family engagement, where mums learned computer skills from their sons and daughters, for example. There are also instances of volunteers becoming involved, some of whom are from an older generation including grandparents, which enabled members not only to make good relationships, but also to share their perspectives and feelings about new technologies.

As Club Tech begins in the UK, this 'wraparound' approach is one aspect that Lisbeth is keen to promote, but she believes there is a 'challenge to transport that to Europe.' Other challenges are deciding what should be in the core curriculum, and how that links with schools, looking to complement rather than supplement what has been learnt already.

The underpinning philosophy of Personalised Learning

The elements that make up Personalised Learning indicate that overall there is a loosening of the strictures of a system that has built up over many years, but that is no longer thought to meet the needs of its client group at the start of the twenty-first century, that is, its pupils, nor the wider society that they will go on to inhabit, serve and mould.

While the elements listed by David Miliband offer a pragmatic approach to professional practice in schools, the underlying concept of Personalised Learning is political and philosophical, rather than educational. It is driven by a notion of equality, of offering every pupil the chance to achieve to the best of their ability, which requires a shift in focus from systemic demands to individual ones. In this way, personalising learning sits very comfortably within the overall Every Child Matters agenda. It is a building block of delivering the five outcomes for all children, and its intention is to place them at the centre of the education endeavour, ensuring the learning needs of each are met.

As the Gilbert Review puts it:

> Personalisation is a matter of moral purpose and social justice: pupils from the most disadvantaged groups are the least likely to achieve well and participate in higher levels of education or training. Personalisation also reflects wider changes in society, which are likely to continue at an increasing rate. Together these present the education system with its most acute challenges. They mean that expectations of what all children and young people should achieve must be raised along with schools' capacity to ensure that outcomes for pupils match those expectations.
>
> (DfES 2006: 7)

One of the biggest issues for schools is that developing an approach based on personalisation will require a change in the way they operate – systems and structures, relationships between adults and children – that have developed over centuries, that are recognised and understood by all stakeholders, and that deliver recognisable outcomes. The risk inherent in change is one that some may be reluctant to make, paradoxically because of a fear that outcomes will change for the worse, when they are intended to improve.

Charlie Leadbetter, a writer on social policy, suggests one way of framing change is to consider the delivery of services as scripts. These need to be rewritten in order to bring about change.

> All public services are delivered according to a script, which directs the parts played by the actors involved. The script for having a meal in a restaurant is: reserve table; arrive at restaurant and be shown to table; examine menu; place order with waiter; food delivered to table; eat; ask for bill; pay; leave. Service innovation comes from rewriting scripts like this so that action unfolds in a different way. So for example, a fast-food restaurant runs on a different script: read menu; place order for food; pay; take food to table yourself; eat; clear away your debris; leave. In a full-service restaurant you eat and then pay, and do very little else. In a fast-food restaurant you pay and then eat, and contribute some of your labour by taking the food to the table and clearing away your mess.
>
> (Leadbetter, 2004)

In this example there is a common core to the script, having a meal, but the processes and the meal itself are very different, with the diner taking more responsibility for the experience, not just being a consumer but having an active role in the event. When such a model is applied to education, there would similarly remain an essential function, the core curriculum, but this could be delivered in different ways, have diverse content, and potentially a range of outcomes each more suited to the learner and their learning journey.

> Personalised learning would provide children with a greater repertoire of possible scripts for how their education could unfold. At the core there would still be a common script – the basic curriculum – but that script could branch out in many ways, to have many different styles and endings.
>
> (*Ibid.*)

With this vision of Personalised Learning, there is a need to shift away from teachers as those who determine what is to be learned and how, to one where they are facilitators, and where pupils are more involved with deciding the process as co-creators and co-designers. Such a change will require mechanisms for pupils to express their preferences – to have a say in their educational experiences. They will need to be able to state clearly their ideas, direction and goals, and to be assured that these will be heard.

As David Miliband said when he was Secretary of State for Education:

> Student voice helps shape provision but because students are not merely educational shoppers in the marketplace; they are creators of their own educational experience; and their voice can help shape provision. Both as a means of engaging students in their own learning – the co-producers of education. And as a means of developing their talents – using their voice to help create choices.
>
> (Miliband, 2004)

If scripts are to be rewritten, then part of the dialogue needs to represent students' views authentically; otherwise, while there may be some change in systemic approaches, the fundamental structure of pupils having education 'done to them' will remain. Only with students' participation can learning become personalised.

> Learner voice is not about learners shouting to be heard, nor is it teachers giving over all their 'powers' to learners. Learner voice is about considering the perspectives and ideas of learners, respecting what everyone has to say, taking risks, sharing, listening, engaging and working together in partnership. Promoting greater learner voice means providing an educational experience where learners are involved in decisions about how, what and when they learn, with whom, and the type of environments in which this occurs.
>
> (Rudd et al., 2006)

Despite the increasingly important emphasis given to the voice of the student, and its role in personalising learning, it is one that is not found within the current inspection framework for schools. That is, there is no specific requirement for Ofsted to evaluate how well schools enable students to have a say in their learning, and in issues affecting the school as a whole. In the current inspection framework, the focus is on the core business of schools and on the five outcomes of the Every Child Matters agenda. This reflects a shift in the framework from one of inspecting the functioning of schools to one of working with schools to help them to make accurate and appropriate evaluations of themselves. In this situation, the inspection is not about whether learning has been personalised, but whether each pupil is enjoying and achieving. Personalisation will be part of the curriculum schools offer that helps to bring about the desired outcomes. The relative relationship of the inspection is one of hearing each school's voice, helping them to articulate their processes and the gains for their pupils.

Academic achievement gives only part of the picture of learners' development. It is much harder to quantify learners' personal development but
this must not be shirked. The Every Child Matters agenda is especially
important to remember when carrying out self-evaluation. Schools can
address the five outcomes for learners separately or by integrating them at
relevant points throughout their evaluation.

(Ofsted 2005a: 7)

When the latest framework for inspection was conceived, the five outcomes
of the Every Child Matters agenda were deliberately threaded throughout it,
rather than being set up as a tick-box checklist. They are intended to permeate
the activities of a school, so similarly need to be integral to the inspection
process. However, each of the outcomes may have a greater emphasis in any
one of the particular sections of the school's Self-Evaluation Framework (now
completed and submitted electronically). Thus the section on achievement and
standards is most likely to examine the school's capacity to support a child's
enjoyment and achievement. Whereas making a positive contribution will fall
under the section on personal development.

As the core business of a school, and therefore the main focus of an inspection,
is education, the overall focus will be on the impact that working towards the
five outcomes has had on learning and on individual learners' development. This
may mean that implementing a Healthy Schools initiative has meant that pupils
are more alert in lessons, or that improvements have been made in interpersonal
relationships and pupils are now better able to work on collaborative tasks.

The individual within the whole

This emphasis on the individual within the collective can be seen in the policy
of inclusion that preceded both Every Child Matters and personalisation.
However, there is a good deal of common resonance running through them all.
While the inclusion agenda was largely seen as having its primary focus on
pupils with special educational needs, its intention was broader than that.
Some pupils were considered to have learning needs that should be met
through something additional to the standard curriculum offering. The aim of
inclusion is to ensure the additional learning needs of all pupils were met,
whether they had learning difficulties or were considered gifted, or perhaps
were from an ethnic minority. This is not to say that at some point a school
can confidently tick a box marked 'inclusion' knowing that everything that
could be done for all its pupils is being done. Inclusion is perceived as a process, a journey rather than a destination, constantly presenting challenges and
involving schools in finding appropriate policies and practices.

Despite its broad remit, it is in the area of special educational needs that the
policy's influence was most felt, as seen by the extract from Hampshire's
Inclusion Policy from 2005, which chooses a 1999 quote from the then

Department for Education and Employment to frame the document: 'We owe all children – whatever their particular needs and circumstances – the opportunity to develop their full potential, to contribute economically, and to play a full part as active citizens.' Immediately, three of the five outcomes from Every Child Matters are evident – enjoying and achieving; making a positive contribution; and achieving economic wellbeing. The policy goes on to outline what is meant by 'inclusion':

> Inclusion is a process, not a fixed state. The term can be used to mean many things including the placement of pupils with SEN in mainstream schools; the participation of all pupils in learning which leads to the highest possible levels of achievement; and the participation of young people in the full range of social experiences and opportunities once they have left school. Thus, for the great majority of children with SEN, there is never any need to consider provision outside the mainstream.
>
> The education of children with special needs is a key challenge for the nation. It is vital to the creation of a fully inclusive society, a society in which all members see themselves as valued for the contribution they make. We owe all children – whatever their particular needs and circumstances – the opportunity to develop their full potential, to contribute economically, and to play a full part as active citizens.
>
> (www3.hants.gov.uk/sen-inclusionpolicy.pdf)

Here there is a clear declaration of the notion that one strand of the agenda is to keep in mainstream schools pupils who otherwise might have been assigned to special schools. Underpinning this policy was a belief that pupils with SEN have a right to be educated alongside their peers – again having echoes in the push for personalisation.

Despite the controversy surrounding this element of the inclusion policy, Ofsted found:

> There was little difference in the quality of provision and outcomes for pupils across primary and secondary mainstream schools and special schools. However, mainstream schools with additionally resourced provision were particularly successful in achieving high outcomes for pupils academically, socially and personally.
>
> (Ofsted, 2006b)

Despite these findings, there has been a noticeable slowdown in the move to close special schools and to include pupils with more profound levels of special needs in mainstream schools, compared with the early years of the policy.

> Contrary to public perception, the move towards the inclusion of children with higher levels of need into mainstream education has progressed very

slowly, with only a gradual reduction in the special school population over the last decade.

(Audit Commission 2002: 18)

This is for many reasons, not least some problems that are identified elsewhere in the report:

Schools have struggled to balance pressures to raise standards of attainment and become more inclusive. This has been reflected in a reluctance to admit and a readiness to exclude some children, particularly those with behavioural difficulties. The existence of separate structures and processes for children with SEN may have allowed their needs to be seen as somehow different – even peripheral – to the core concerns of our system of education.

(*Ibid.*: 2)

It may be that highlighting the special educational needs of these pupils meant that they came to be seen as so different. One of the methods used to ensure they receive the support they need in order to achieve is the Individual Education Plan.

Strategies employed to enable the child to progress should be recorded within an Individual Education Plan (IEP). ... The IEP should include information about:
- the short-term targets set for or by the child
- the teaching strategies to be used
- the provision to be put in place
- when the plan is to be reviewed
- success and/or exit criteria
- outcomes (to be recorded when IEP is reviewed).

(DfES, 2001: para 5:50)

This approach of determining tight targets for pupils' progress, then allocating resources to help to achieve them, has spread beyond pupils needing support for their additional learning needs. In most mainstream schools that don't select by ability, there is reckoned to be approximately 20 per cent of the population who will have a special need of some sort. There will typically be another 10 per cent who could be deemed 'gifted and talented' in some way. When schools and authorities begin to think about inclusion in terms broader than simply pupils with special educational needs, the latter group come into focus, and often receive attention to provide individual planning in a similar way. Beyond them are also pupils from ethnic minorities, including traveller groups. And then there are those who may be on the periphery of the education system, which can include those in care, the socially isolated, and those whose behaviour is challenging to the degree that they may become excluded.

There can be a planning process for all of these. Looked-after children should have an Education Plan as part of their Care Plan. This will consider their development in the broadest sense, so may include out-of-school activities – a sports club or youth group such as the Scouts – to help with learning social skills.

Pupils who are at risk of exclusion will be the subject of a Pastoral Support Programme. This will outline expectations for a pupil's behaviour (often as a contract between pupil, school and home), how this will be monitored, and the resources allocated to help make it a success. This will usually involve school staff who are part of the pastoral team, such as a learning mentor or head of year. These pupils may also have an IEP in place at the same time – again naming adult support, only here from the learning support staff, which may include a teaching assistant or specialist teacher.

The trend for target-setting has continued to spread, is one way in which schools are beginning to implement Personalised Learning. Many secondary schools regularly have days (either at the beginning of each term or at half-yearly intervals) when students attend, usually with a parent or carer, and set personal targets with a form tutor. In this way, every child is intended to have some aspects of their individual learning needs identified and, through the regular cycle of meetings, monitored. Although there may, in reality, be little impact on the pupil's learning experiences.

The role for ICT is to provide a way of recording and monitoring this information. There are several packages available to help. A number are specifically for IEPs, such as IEPWriter[3] and IEP Complete,[4] and others are built into widely used systems for whole-school management such as SIMS.[5] There is also always the option of creating a bespoke system using generic products such as Microsoft Excel or Microsoft Access.

Another role is to provide timely and accurate information for teachers, pupils and parents to inform such discussions. Again, these can be supported by management information systems. These are now beginning to be linked in to schools' learning platforms so that marking and assessment can be updated more quickly, and ultimately parents and pupils will have access to view these results, and their impact on overall achievement, just as quickly. It is a means of ensuring parents have up-to-date information on their children that has the backing of the government,

> Speaking at an event today on the government's Parent Know How programme, which aims to develop new and innovative ways of helping parents access information and support, Balls said research shows parents prefer informal chats with school staff instead of parents evenings and want to get information on their children's progress online.
>
> (*The Guardian*, 7 May 2008)

The move from a policy of inclusion to one of personalisation represents a shift in focus, from ensuring that particular children have access to the education they deserve, to one where all children are included in that bracket – from one where some additional label was required to gain entry to a group for additional consideration, to one where the focus is on the needs of all children. Literally, that Every Child Matters, and that all children deserve individual thought and attention. This is also reflected in the National Curriculum and its Inclusion Statement:

> Schools have a responsibility to provide a broad and balanced curriculum for all pupils. The National Curriculum is the starting point for planning a school curriculum that meets the specific needs of individuals and groups of pupils.
> (English National Curriculum Statutory Inclusion Statement, 2000)

The Inclusion Statement sets out three principles that are essential to developing a more inclusive curriculum:

A. Setting suitable learning challenges
B. Responding to pupils' diverse learning needs
C. Overcoming potential barriers to learning and assessment for individuals and groups of pupils.

(Ibid.)

There are many challenges for teachers in making these principles a day-to-day reality. 'Special educational needs' can cover pupils with a wide range of learning difficulties, all of which will require additional resources. For instance, some pupils who are deemed to have social, emotional and behavioural difficulties may not require support in order to learn academically, but to engage appropriately with teachers and their fellow pupils. Similarly, other pupils may require the help of a teaching assistant because of a physical disability – to record work on their behalf – rather than to scaffold the learning itself.

The paradox of standards

As seen previously, much of the tension generated by the push for greater inclusion in schools was brought about by a simultaneous push to raise standards. This has seen the introduction of first the Literacy and Numeracy hours (which later merged to form the Primary Strategy), followed by the Key Stage 3 strategy and the ongoing reform of the examination system. Alongside this has been the testing regime that sees children being uniformly assessed across England at the end of Key Stages 1, 2 and 3, by tests that have come to be known as SATs. Schools and local authorities are set annual targets for the outcomes. The ongoing controversy around publication of the results in league tables continues only in England, all other home nations having abandoned them. These are just one way of making judgements about schools, the other main method being the ever-evolving Ofsted inspection frameworks.

There is an obvious dichotomy between an agenda that seeks to raise the achievement levels in schools and aggregates the results to demonstrate how well they are doing it, and one that aims to increase the numbers of pupils with special educational needs in mainstream institutions.

> Schools feel pulled in opposite directions by pressures to achieve ever-better academic results and to become more inclusive. National performance tables and targets fail to reflect the achievement of many children with SEN. Government needs to find a way of recognising and celebrating the achievements of these pupils and their teachers, often against considerable odds.
>
> (Audit Commission, 2002)

Any perceived reluctance by schools to open their doors fully to pupils considered to have special educational needs may be understood in the light of the impact on their overall results – it may lower overall scores, and need a high level of resourcing that could be put towards raising levels for other groups. However, there are mechanisms in place to ameliorate these issues. Pupils can be disapplied from the National Curriculum, in part or in full, if it is felt that their needs can otherwise be better met (an option that is seldom taken as the National Curriculum has a large degree of flexibility built into it). They can also be withdrawn from SATs tests under some circumstances.

However, in hard-pressed schools the moral and ethical imperatives that drive the inclusion agenda may be tempered by pragmatic ones – to meet targets and improve ratings in league tables. This issue has largely been addressed through the use of contextual value-added (CVA) factors when making judgements (see Chapter Three). These acknowledge that simply comparing schools by overall performance is too crude a measure – that pupils' performance is affected by many factors, and that the pupil intake in a school in a commuter suburb will be different from that in a rural farming community or an inner-city estate. Contextual value-added takes the various elements that may have an impact on learning and factors them into the calculations, so that the judgement becomes one not of whether a school has done well because of high scores in a league table, but of how well pupils have achieved given the context from which they come, and therefore what might be expected of them. In this way, it is possible to evaluate a school that is considered high-performing and find that, given the profile of the student group, the results should be higher yet.

The current factors taken in to account for CVA can be seen here in the DCSF guidance:

> When calculating a school's CVA measure, we take into account pupil level factors that have been observed to impact on a pupil performance –

prior attainment, gender, ethnicity, age in year, SEN status, free school meals status, first language, whether pupil is or has been in care, mobility and a rating from the Income Deprivation Affecting Children Index (IDACI).

(DCSF, 2007a: para 4)

The elements taken into account have a different degree of impact on the calculations, and are seen to interrelate and interact. Prior attainment is a means of tracking performance over the course of a pupil's school career. Some elements take into account differing rates of development, for example, gender recognises that girls develop more quickly than boys. 'Age in year' recognises that the range of ages in any one pupil cohort can vary by up to 364 days – a significant amount, the impact of which diminishes over the course of a school career. The impact of deprivation is seen in 'free school meals' and the inclusion of the IDACI rating, while the importance of stability for achievement is seen in the use of factors for having been in care, and for mobility – moving between schools at times other than the standard ones. The algorithms that balance these factors and the relationships between them are complicated, and are possible to achieve only through the use of ICT.

When these factors are taken into account, each school is given a CVA rating normed on 100 – a score higher than this means they are exceeding expectations, a lower score means the converse.[6]

Finding the individual in the sum

The use of ICT is integral to promoting a system whereby an evaluation of a school's effectiveness can be based on the performance of the particular profile of each individual, rather than simply the sum of them all.

In the first instance, it provides the database to hold the information. The national system developed for all schools, and used by Ofsted, is known as Reporting and Analysis for Improvement through School Self-Evaluation (RAISEonline; see Chapter Three). Here data are uploaded centrally and shared with schools and local authorities through the internet. This makes a number of options available. Information can be downloaded to have additional data added; it can also be interrogated by running queries and reports, in a number of ways and at a number of levels. As well as showing the aggregate achievement totals for the whole school, it can also do this for particular groups, and can offer comparisons focusing on differences between boys and girls, or on ethnicity, for example. It can also show progress of pupils with special needs, to demonstrate how effective the school has been in raising their achievement and meeting their needs over time, not just as individuals, but as a group. The database is currently being refined to do this more effectively by including the P scales (the National Curriculum levels for pupils who are 'pre-National Curriculum').

As the basis of the information is the national testing structure, it is also possible to interrogate individual answers to particular questions, or the questions themselves, to show gaps in understanding; or for whole groups, areas of teaching that need to become more rigorous.

For pupils on the P scales, it can be difficult to determine what progress has been made, as they may move forward only in small steps. For this reason, a number of specialist recording systems have emerged. One such is Performance Indicators for Value-Added Target Setting (PIVATS), developed by Lancashire County Council. In this system, each of the eight levels of the P scales are split into three further levels, with suggestions as to how progress between them can be identified. A numerical score is given to each step and, through an online service, progress can be charted.

Because of the degree of flexibility that ICT offers, data can be manipulated to provide a more sophisticated understanding of both individual pupils' progress and that of the school as a whole. Within this, controls can be built in to accommodate the various backgrounds and experiences of each child, to demonstrate how these are reflected in the overall outcomes. Without such systems, it would be very hard to show not only the achievement of the individual, but also how much the school has contributed to it. Through these means, school accountability can be developed from a crude total of the output of tests, to one where the outcomes for every child count, and can be identified within the whole. This can also help provide a means of ensuring the school is providing an effective education for each of them.

New tools for learning

As we can now focus more sharply on the learning performance of each individual pupil, we can also offer them a greater range of learning opportunities that are no longer necessarily located within the traditional boundaries of schools – those of time and place. By implementing a learning platform, schools can provide any time, any place, learning.

In order to support schools in selecting and using a learning platform, Becta has developed a framework that includes a detailed technical specification and online guidance for schools (see Chapter Three). Becta has also issued simple, straightforward guidance setting out what a learning platform is:

> There are four keys areas of functionality, all of which will contribute to a Personalised Learning experience:
>
> - Communication tools: email, messaging or discussion boards, to enable dialogue between peers and mentors
> - Individual working space, to enable the creation and sharing of learning resources which can be accessed online, outside lesson time and from any location

- Management tools so teachers can manage e-learning resources and assess, monitor and track individual and group progress
- Access that is safe and secure, at any time and from any internet-enabled device.

(Becta, 2007b)

These elements of functionality can all be found in various systems and software, both on school networks and freely available on the internet. The communication tools are in very regular use, through email, messaging arrangements such as MSN and Skype, and message boards – whether for specialist groups or those providing feedback on sites such as Blogger or Flickr. There are also plenty of examples of collaborative tools. Google Docs,[7] for instance, allows multiple users to contribute to one output. Another site, with a more educational focus, that allows such working is just2easy.[8] Here students can choose to make their creative endeavours available to others to edit and to develop further. As discussed previously, the potential for recording performance data continues to develop and become more defined.

However, providing all elements in a combined, interrelated system that is both secure and easily available online is what brings these together into a learning platform. The collaborative working tools in the public domain cannot provide the certainty that work will remain unaltered in an unintended way, which is necessary for schools to have the confidence to use them. Nor are online messaging systems considered sufficiently secure for teachers to use them confidently with pupils. The tools have been brought together and packaged for educational purposes, along with a space to be used as an e-portfolio.

Although the technology now exists for these ways of working to be implemented, a number of issues still need to be addressed. In the first instance, there is the question of how, when and by whom they will be used. There is an assumption that all pupils are confident and familiar with such tools. However, this may well not be the case, and is undoubtedly not so for all teachers. Second, pupils need to feel comfortable with methods of communication that they have adopted for personal, social use being appropriated for educational purposes. As with the use of computer games in education, this may be seen as 'uncool'.

In their paper 'Taking up online opportunities? Children's uses of the internet for education, communication and participation', Livingstone and Bober (2004) distinguish between two predominant types of internet use: for information and for communication. While they found that most children were comfortable with the former, it was only those who were frequent (daily) users who were confident with the latter. They also found that even when using the web for research purposes, there were still concerns about evaluating the validity of information.

At present, we have found that although the Internet has already become important in children's and young people's lives as an information medium to support school work, it is not seen as a wholly unproblematic learning tool. Young people encounter difficulties with searching the Web, with the critical evaluation of website contents, and with a range of other online skills, and these in turn appear due to the patchy educational support they have received in Internet literacy teaching. More educational support on Internet-related skills, especially going beyond basic skills to encourage development of critical literacy skills online, is urgently needed. Attention is also needed to the distinction between information-based and communication-based uses of the Internet.

(Livingstone and Bober, 2004)

Martin Johnson is also wary of the confidence placed in pupils to negotiate the internet and extract the appropriate information. His solution is to provide much closer support than is often in evidence currently, considering the internet to be a vast repository of information that pupils need help to navigate.

Many library users sometimes wish for guidance through the available material and how to retrieve it. Pupils, of course, need much more guidance. They need support and reassurance, they need human feedback, they need help in selecting material. Since most websites are designed for adults, staff are needed to catalogue and develop material to fill gaps.

(Johnson, 2004: 10)

As a resource, Livingstone and Bober found that 'children and young people themselves are far more excited by the Internet as a communication medium,' and they believe this usage is often restricted in schools and at home. However, they also state that 'it is through online communication that students explore, experiment and so gain a wider range of Internet-based skills, confidence and expertise that may carry over into traditionally defined "educational" uses' (Livingstone and Bober, 2004).

If the use of learning platforms in schools is to be successful, it is not just the impact on traditional uses that needs consideration, but also the use of the communication skills themselves: the adoption of elements of students' lifestyles – electronic communication and sharing – within the educational domain. Such a shift is part of a trend that Livingstone and Bovill (1999) detect when they talk of 'blurring of boundaries between traditionally distinct activities such as information, education, work and entertainment', and again of those 'between producer/consumer, work/leisure, entertainment/information.'

It is happening already

While the use of the internet is facilitating this blurring of previous distinctions between different aspects of life, and purposeful learning is taking place, this is not reflected in what is happening in schools.

Rather than harnessing the technologies that are already fully integrated into young people's daily lives, schools primarily have a 'battening down the hatches' approach.

(Green and Hannon, 2007: 24)

However, Green and Hannon go on to suggest that the answer is not in the wholesale accommodation of external learning experiences into schools. 'We argue that the answer does not lie in absorbing informal learning into the formal school environment, but in isolating positive elements of informal learning and creating spaces and places to build on these in more formal settings.' (*Ibid.*) Such a shift could be seen in the implementation of learning platforms, where positive elements – of communication, collaboration and creativity – are being brought into play in a way similar to their use in informal situations. The adoption of these tools within schools, though, will also require a recognition of the additional learning they can bring about.

As an example of what can be learned through use of the internet, Green and Hannon give the example of players of a multi-player, online game.

To be an effective World of Warcraft guildmaster one needs to be adept at many skills: attracting, evaluating and recruiting new members; creating apprenticeship programmes; orchestrating group strategy; and managing disputes. All of these skills are readily welcomed in the modern workplace, and they are set to become even more valuable.

(*Ibid.*)

They go on to suggest that these are skills that it would be difficult to acquire without the use of such a medium, arguing that 'the idea that they can be taught in any traditional sense with a teacher standing at the front of a classroom is disputable.' They also state that in order to support this learning, it is necessary to provide 'a space to reflect on it, galvanise and develop it so students can recognise and transfer those skills in new situations and contexts.'

Beyond gaming, there are some attempts to use the new, virtual situations that the internet provides to create structured learning opportunities. One developing area of the web is the provision of virtual worlds where users adopt avatars in order to live and interact. The leader in this area, Second Life (see Chapter Two), has developed Teen Second Life to try and prevent young people joining the adult environment, which is apparently tightly regulated and reserved for those over 18. The Teen version is similarly tightly regulated and is available only to those between the ages of 13 and 17; the only adults allowed access to this area are staff of Linden Labs, the creators. This does not preclude its use for educational purposes: it is possible to purchase virtual private islands that can have their access rights limited, so that adult educators can create learning experiences while having their own movement restricted to this one area.

A number of projects have begun to use Teen Second Life, either developing them for schools, or involving schools in their use. In the first category, VITAL Lab at Ohio University[9] has created a number of projects for schools – and others, including the general public – to make use of. The Interactive Science Lab, for instance, provides simulations of experiments: some are set up as games with scoring; others replicate famous experiments from history. In Fruit Fly Genetics, students decide what colours should be the dominant and recessive genes. Then they allow them to breed, before knocking them out to quantify how the traits have been passed on.

Other uses of Teen Second Life have been projects such as Skoolaborate.[10] This has brought together nine schools from Australia, New Zealand, Japan and the USA to work together in a virtual world, putting into practice skills and values inculcated through their schools' curricula. In one instance, to practise literacy and communication skills – particularly for those for whom English is not their first language – the students created avatars, then were given a list of questions with which to interview each other. The project has a number of aims, many of them concerned with global learning, citizenship, and being active and enabled members of the global community. These include: 'Develop intercultural understanding in schools and their community members', and 'Have young people work together on innovative projects which engage them in unaccustomed forms of action that create understanding of differences and promote conflict resolution skills between individuals and groups'. As well as these objectives, which focus on output, there are also some that focus on processes, such as 'Build the capacity of school students and their teachers in digital media and learning'.

The latter is one of the areas where learning in schools may be falling behind what children and young people are already doing in their leisure time. This is happening for several reasons. First, some of the ways in which young people are developing their computer skills fall outside the school curriculum; second, teachers may not have the skills to teach all aspects of ICT, and finally, this is a fast-changing field. One response has been for young people to learn autonomously using tuition materials and expertise found through the internet.

An example of this is secondary-age pupils who are using materials provided by Microsoft to improve their skills in developing computer games outside school. While game-building has been an activity in which enthusiastic adolescent gamers have been indulging for some years – mainly by modifying existing video games using resources bundled in with them – it is now possible for them to use the professional language developed by Microsoft called XNA. The company provides home-use licensing, a developers' forum and a place to showcase the results.[11] One of the attractions of the language, apart from the quality of the results, is that their creations can be played on the Xbox console platform.

While the attraction of making and playing games is understandable, there are also teenagers who are learning full-scale programming languages online.

Tutorials have been created for a growing group who want to learn to use tools including C# and Visual Basic.[12] Although there may only be a small group that have the motivation and interest to pursue learning in their own time in this way, it is indicative of the ways in which ICT is opening up new fields for learning, and new ways of studying and acquiring knowledge, that have yet to find a place in the mainstream school curriculum and structure. This is particularly so as the majority of qualifications in schools are focused on the application of ICT skills, rather than traditional programming or computer science.

For those who do not want to work at that level of programming, or for younger children, there are plenty of free, downloadable programs whereby they, too, can become involved in creating their own games, animations, multimedia outputs and interactive events. Two examples come from MIT: StarLogo[13] and Scratch.[14]

The first of these is a development of the programming language Logo, originally developed by Seymour Papert[15] (along with Wally Feurzeig) in 1967 to explore constructivist ways of learning through problem-solving with children. It is a freely available program, and has led to a number of variants (some estimates are up to 170), including commercial versions such as MicroWorlds.[16] StarLogo is one such development, which remains open-source and so can be freely used and developed. In this version, the software is intended to model systems where there is no leader or coordinator, such as flocks of birds, or a snooker break. By creating a number of individual 'turtles' (on-screen, programmable devices), each programmed to work in similar ways but also to respond to each other, such systems can be modelled and explored.

> StarLogo is a programmable modelling environment for exploring the workings of decentralized systems – systems that are organized without an organizer, coordinated without a coordinator. With StarLogo, you can model (and gain insights into) many real-life phenomena, such as bird flocks, traffic jams, ant colonies, and market economies.
>
> (http://education.mit.edu/starlogo)

Scratch is similar in its method of development – an open-source program that developers can build on further – but provides different learning opportunities. Using a drag-and-drop interface, users can build platform games (think Pacman), animations or interactive art works. These can be posted on the Scratch website for others to enjoy. However, they can also be edited, adapted and developed further by other users. The site provides information on how to use the program, but there is also a thriving discussion group offering solutions to problems, and hints and tips on how to achieve the desired result. This is a developing community of practice, which is taking the tools provided and building a range of creations, supporting each other and drawing on expertise as it is needed to move forward. The program is available for teachers to download and use with their classes (see Chapter Two for an example of this), and it is being widely used outside the formal curriculum. But the skills being learned – of logically constructing sequences of commands, with ongoing problem-solving, to create real-life outputs such as games and animations – are applicable within the curriculum. There are very few routes for students working in this way to have their achievements accredited, although this situation is beginning to change.

Recognising new learning

The system for accrediting learning has been a subject of much debate in recent years. There have been plenty of suggestions that the improvements in exam results are due to papers getting easier, and there is a desire to develop the options for vocational learning, while trying to improve its comparative status alongside traditional qualifications that are perceived as more academic. The Tomlinson Report[17] has brought this into focus, and the introduction of diplomas is seeking a way of resolving the tensions. Among the reforms have been some that address the impact of new technologies on our lives, both in our digital outputs and in our opportunities for digital communication. These range from approaches that retain much of the structure of more traditionally recognisable qualifications, to those that are attempting to reflect the changes in skills and communication afforded by recent advances in new technologies.

One aim of these new qualifications is to provide pupils with choices in the path they follow to obtain them, to give them an element of personalisation. As well as a number of optional courses within them, they will also be taught in different locations across an authority, and ICT will be used to link up students and to provide access to expertise – through video-conferencing, for instance.

The Diploma in Digital Applications (DiDA) is one such qualification from the Edexcel exam board.[18] This consists of a number of modules, one compulsory and several optional, which can be taken at both level one and level two. To achieve the DiDA, candidates have to complete four units, although if they complete fewer they can still gain a Certificate in Digital Applications (CiDA) for two, or an Award in Digital Applications (AiDA) for just the mandatory one.

In the initial versions of the qualification there are only four units, so no real choice in the optional ones for those seeking to gain a DiDA. These are: Using ICT (mandatory), Multimedia, Graphics, and ICT in enterprise. While the content for all these has some resonance with that of existing level one and two qualifications – such as GCSE Applied ICT – one essential difference is the use of an e-portfolio (see Chapter Two) for recording and submitting work. It is paper-free.

The qualification is also due to become more representative of the new products of ICT, and the necessary skills to create them, with the introduction of the Active Web and Games Authoring. The first of these is concerned with interactivity and the internet, while the second will be the first qualification at this level specifically to accredit games authoring as an examined subject.

Case study – DiDA and making games

Not only is the DiDA a new qualification, it is also a new approach to qualifications, an attempt to move away from what might be perceived as staid or static. 'We want students to have fun,' Ann Weidmann, Qualifications Leader for ICT at Edexcel explains, 'The problem with the GNVQ is it's become a sort of sausage machine. I want DiDA to be a broader experience. I see it as learning a life skill. Having done a DiDA unit, they can see connections between that activity and what they do in their broader lives.'

Like playing computer games, something DiDA will need to reflect. Not only could computer games soon be submitted in the e-portfolio (once file formats are agreed), but a specialist games development unit is planned. Ann Weidmann sees two possible problems. The first is that 'Once you move away from office applications, a lot of teachers get scared,' so staff would need training not just in using the software, but also in understanding and assessing a medium of which they may have little experience. The second is 'the availability of suitable authoring software for level two students.'

The latter difficulty is no longer a real issue since Immersive Education[19] released MissionMaker, software specifically designed for school students to make games. For a start, the environment is created by dragging and dropping settings onto a grid; a click of the mouse and this becomes a 360°, texture-rich, three-dimensional location. From here, props and characters can be added, all capable of being programmed to respond to various triggers as players progress through the game. Artefacts can be gathered and used, health and wealth depleted and restored, and problems and solutions embedded – just like in the real thing. With the capacity to add information through posters, sound and video, this could offer the first opportunity to bring games into the DiDA through the multimedia module.

Students could set players a challenge – to save a local character or landmark, perhaps. Progress through the game would not happen without them having used particular information gathered by reading posters, watching video clips and picking up souvenirs. This is a process of solving problems and overcoming obstacles, and gathering and using information, presented in an innovative way. Which raises a final problem – might this be so different that the only people qualified to mark it will be not examiners, but gamers?

A more radical approach?

A qualification that has moved on completely from more traditional content is iMedia from OCR,[20] which suggests that it will 'attract those already working in the field or interested in working as web designers, graphic artists, multimedia producers, animators, sound designers and storyboarders'. These are all forms of employment that have existed for some years, but are now becoming sufficiently established that school pupils can aspire to joining their ranks. The content here is more clearly divorced from that of traditional, school-based qualifications, with a focus entirely on digital creations and outputs. There is still a conventional aspect, though, in terms of the content and structure being targeted at skills drawn from, and contributing to, working life post-school.

One qualification that attempts to acknowledge and accredit skills and capabilities acquired through more informal learning, developed with the use of new technologies, is the Digital Cre8or[21] from the British Computer Society. This seeks to take informal learning, in the form of the creativity demonstrated by the use of electronic media for the internet, and give recognition to the range of techniques and abilities necessary to produce and publish in this way. This qualification has two sets of elements – creative units and sharing units – to reflect the way in which digital media are both constructed and shared. To complete the qualification, it is necessary to show capability in both sections: both to create an electronic entity and to share it with others. Categories are:

Creative units
- Understand, capture and manipulate digital audio
- Understand, capture and manipulate digital still images
- Understanding moving image language
- Understand, capture and manipulate digital video
- Digital storytelling with animation

Sharing units
- Sharing digital media on optical media such as DVDs
- Sharing digital media on the web
- Sharing digital media using presentations.

In order to gain the qualification, candidates have to complete four units in total, with at least one from each section. Evidence might include taking a film on a mobile phone and posting it on YouTube, although there does need to be both a degree of understanding about the composition of an image, and technical competency such as considerations of file size and format.

It is possible that even new qualifications – based on activities that have emerged only recently, and that acknowledge and accredit the sorts of informal learning pupils are undertaking beyond school, but which have not yet been formally embraced – are not going far enough. Marc Prensky's argument that new technologies are changing the brain itself, and the way it works, suggests that we need ways to test the competences and capabilities that are now being developed. He lists a number of such skills.

> For example, thinking skills enhanced by repeated exposure to computer games and other digital media include reading visual images as representations of three-dimensional space (representational competence), multi-dimensional visual–spatial skills, mental maps, 'mental paper folding' (i.e. picturing the results of various origami-like folds in your mind without actually doing them), 'inductive discovery' (i.e. making observations, formulating hypotheses and figuring out the rules governing the behaviour of a dynamic representation), 'attentional deployment' (such as monitoring multiple locations simultaneously), and responding faster to expected and unexpected stimuli.
>
> (Prensky, 2001: 4)

Soft skills, hard to measure

While these new skills are beginning to be acknowledged and accredited, there are others that may prove very difficult to measure, but that are considered crucial to meet the demands of twenty-first century living. These include skills of discrimination, analysis, cooperation, team working, empathy and problem-solving – those that are focused on thinking, reflection and relationships, often referred to as 'soft skills'.

One that is seen as crucial, but is seldom formally acknowledged, is that of being confident and competent users of the world-wide web, for finding and sharing information and for communicating with others. We also need to be sure that, as well as being competent users of the internet, pupils are able to do so safely. Here the emphasis is not on the role of ICT in sharing information in order to meet the desired outcome of staying safe, but in ensuring that when children are using it, they can remain so. The recent Byron Review[22] into 'the risks to children from exposure to potentially harmful or inappropriate material on the internet and in video games' gives a balanced response to the problems. This is reflected in the comment that ' ... the potential risks online are closely correlated with potential benefits. Data is beginning to reveal risks to young people in terms of increased exposure to sexually inappropriate content, contributions to negative beliefs and attitudes, stranger danger, cyberbullying and access to inappropriate sites which may promote harmful behaviours.' (DCSF, 2008c: para. 8)

In response to these threats, the review proposes a three-pronged approach. The first objective is to reduce the availability of harmful material, which is made easier because the majority of material accessed on the internet comes from a small number of popular sites (such as Wikipedia or the BBC). Second, parents should know how to restrict access, perhaps through the use of specialist software, and children should be taught to monitor their own activity to protect themselves. Finally, we need to build children's resilience to exposure to inappropriate material – it is unrealistic to expect that exposure will never happen, so they need to know how to deal with it when it does.

To meet these three objectives, two strategies are proposed, one for regulation, the other focused on information and education. While a large part of the responsibility for the latter will fall on schools, the role of parents 'is also recognised – although the disparity in skills between them and their offspring is clearly an issue.

> However, while most children may have better technical skills than their parents, this does not necessarily translate into a greater understanding of e-safety. Research shows that, not only do the most skilled young people fail to avoid online risks, but that their risky encounters increase with increased use. (Livingstone and Bober, 2005)
>
> *(Ibid.*: para. 5.22)

So if parents are not in a position to provide their children with boundaries for staying safe, the onus falls on young people themselves to be aware of both the possible problems, and the flaws and faults of a largely unregulated information system where anyone can have a presence and offer up material.

> This highlights a need to provide children with not only the skills, but also the knowledge and understanding to use new technology safely. There is much evidence to suggest that younger people, despite their confidence, lack the wider competencies to protect themselves. For example, 38% of pupils have said that they trust most of the information on the internet, while 21% have admitted to copying something from the internet and handing it in as their own. (Livingstone and Bober, 2005)
>
> *(Ibid.*: para. 5.23)

These skills – being able to assess information, question its validity, reflect on its accuracy, and be aware of issues of perspective, point of view, bias and prejudice – are necessary for coping with the information-rich environment that ICT is providing. The skills needed include being able to search effectively for the necessary information, then analyse it objectively, consider its accuracy, reliability and validity, and empathise with the provider – whether sympathetic to them or not – before using it appropriately to make a case, develop an argument or illustrate a point. All these skills are contained within the latest revision of the National Curriculum, along with explicit references to e-safety. Given that the curriculum content is secure, Byron believes the focus for schools needs to be on the adults involved in delivering that curriculum – not just teachers, but teaching assistants and also parents – in order that 'E-safety and media literacy should be embedded across teaching and learning, not "bolted on".' (*Ibid.*: para. 5.92)

The kinds of skills that would be encompassed by 'media literacy' are those of working effectively with information – knowing how to find it and how to evaluate it:

> The speed of change in the world, the diverse sources of information and media we encounter daily are making what you know less important than how adept you are at knowing where to look. The skills that we need revolve around distinguishing sources of information that are trustworthy from those that lack credibility and being able to filter, summarise and critically analyse a vast range of different sources.
>
> (Green and Hannon, 2007: 57)

There is consensus, then, that children need specific skills in order to operate on the web. Byron emphasises that e-safety should be taught in schools, and finds that the broader skills of media literacy are already in the curriculum. The issue remains of how these skills of researching, communicating and collaborating remotely are to be developed in children and young people. While the National Curriculum outlines what they should learn, it is not prescriptive about how this should happen (although the Qualifications and Curriculum Authority has developed schemes of work across all subjects to support schools in doing this). However, as shown later in this chapter, there are a number of approaches to developing a skills-based, rather than a content-based, curriculum. Within these, the skills of harnessing the power of the internet for learning are recognised and promoted.

> If we want to unlock the considerable opportunity for collaborative learning offered by the internet then we must train children how to operate effectively and safely in such communities and empower them with the authority to feed their informal learning back into their school.
>
> (Buckley, 2007: 35)

The skills and capacities needed to function safely and effectively on the internet are not the only ones considered necessary for those undergoing schooling now and in the future. There has been some official focus on these skills in recent years. The Leitch Review of Skills[23] talks of the need to raise skill levels for the future prosperity of the country, but does not outline what these skills are. Whereas *2020 Vision*, the review of Personalised Learning undertaken by Christine Gilbert immediately before becoming Her Majesty's Chief Inspector of Schools, outlined a number of them. These are sometimes misleadingly called 'soft skills', and include:

- being able to communicate orally at a high level
- reliability, punctuality and perseverance

- knowing how to work with others in a team
- knowing how to evaluate information critically
- taking responsibility for, and being able to manage, one's own learning and developing the habits of effective learning
- knowing how to work independently without close supervision
- being confident and able to investigate problems and find solutions
- being resilient in the face of difficulties
- being creative, inventive, enterprising and entrepreneurial.

(DfES 2006: 10)

The report notes that skills such as these are becoming increasingly important, not just to employers, but also in further and higher education, possibly more so than knowing and understanding specific aspects of a subject. They go on to point out that:

> However, the National Curriculum gives them relatively little weight and they are measured, recorded and reported inadequately by national tests and most public examinations. As a result, they are in danger of being neglected by teachers and undervalued by pupils and their parents at a time when they matter more than ever.
>
> (*Ibid.*)

One response to this perceived disjunct between the curriculum and the skills necessary for study and employment in the twenty-first century has been a review of the secondary National Curriculum, which comes into effect in September 2008. This is seeking to strike a balance between subject content and the skills necessary for learning, and those needed for the economic good of the country.

> The strong focus on the curriculum aims should help to ensure that young people leave school equipped with the knowledge, skills and attitudes to cope with life and work in the 21st century. In particular, they will be more able to meet the demands of employers, who are looking for young people with good functional skills, are flexible, and are able to work well in teams, solve problems and make decisions. A coherent approach to personal development will help all learners to grow into mature, independent and fulfilled adults.[24]

There is also an overt statement on the aims of the curriculum that closely reflects those of the Every Child Matters outcomes.

The curriculum should enable all young people to become:
- successful learners who enjoy learning, make progress and achieve
- confident individuals who are able to live safe, healthy and fulfilling lives
- responsible citizens who make a positive contribution to society.[25]

These changes in the curriculum will affect all secondary schools in the country. However, there have already been initiatives in recent years that have attempted to address the issue of developing the curriculum and making it more engaging. An example is the Excellence in Cities programme,[26] which ran from 1999 to 2006. This had seven strands, one of which was to establish a number of City Learning Centres. These are technologically rich venues (attached to schools, although largely independent of them) that offer opportunities for teaching and learning with ICT that otherwise are not available. They have a brief to be innovative and experimental, to explore possibilities, and inspire practitioners and pupils.

> City Learning Centres (CLCs), of which over 100 have been established since 2000, are designed to enhance the whole curriculum using high quality ICT facilities. Their aims are to raise educational standards and skill levels and thus promote employability and social inclusion. Each Partnership has a small number of CLCs, designed to be resources shared not only by schools but also by the community more generally. The aim was that each CLC should provide state-of-the-art ICT-based learning opportunities for the pupils at the host school, for pupils at a network of surrounding schools, and for the wider community.
>
> (Kendall *et al.*, 2005: para. 7.6)

While funding through the Excellence in Cities programme has finished, City Learning Centres have continued and are now supported from other resources, such as the 14–19 strategy. The push for educational innovation through ICT has also emerged in another recent initiative, Building Schools for the Future, which is spending £25 billion over 15 years to refurbish or rebuild every secondary school in the country. This is running alongside, and is additional to, the Academies programme, which has a different funding stream but shares many of the aims – creating establishments fit for the new century.

Building Schools for the Future

In order to participate in the Building Schools for the Future scheme, local authorities and schools have to demonstrate their vision for education in their area by preparing a number of documents, including a Strategy for Change that outlines the current situation in the school and authority, and how it will move forward through Building Schools for the Future. This entails developing a vision for the future, which must show how, among other things, it is intended to 'deliver personalised learning to ensure that every pupil is fully stretched and can access a broad curriculum that best suits their needs and talents' and 'ensure effective integration of education and other services through Every Child Matters' (DCSF, 2008a: 45). The role of ICT is integral to Building Schools for the Future, with a large proportion of the funding going into it.

Information and Communications Technology (ICT) has immense potential to change both teaching and learning, encouraging individual learning
programmes tailored to individual pupil needs and allowing learning to
take place outside of school sites and school hours. Roughly 10% of
Building Schools for the Future funding is allocated to ICT, reflecting its
importance.

(*Ibid.*: 39)

Although these government initiatives, which are changing the educational
landscape – and which overtly state their belief in the role of ICT – are
moving forward, it will take time for them to become embedded. Ideas and
innovations from other quarters are moving more quickly.

Following not leading

While government-funded and -promoted initiatives are beginning to bring
about change, to some degree these changes, in both the content of the
National Curriculum and its method of delivery, are following rather than
leading a trend. Several manifestations have already emerged of how the curriculum can be made more relevant to educational needs, now and in the
future. Some focus on delivery, on pedagogy, on how the curriculum is taught,
ranging from changing teaching styles to empowering students in the process,
and giving them more responsibility for their own learning. Others focus on
the curriculum content, what it is that needs to be learned, and how this can
be done while employing innovative approaches – all of them, to varying
degrees, involve the use of ICT to achieve their aims. What follows is an
overview of five such innovative models of the curriculum.

New curricular models

The range of models that have emerged in recent years varies in a number of
ways: in the focus they place on the respective roles of teacher and student; in
the place of the established curriculum; in the role of ICT; and in the changes
in institutional organisation involved. Below are a number of examples of such
models, ranging from those focused on shifts in pedagogy to make current
practice more effective, to shifts in the school experience of young people.
They are:

- Accelerated Learning – the focus is on pedagogy, on what the teacher does.
  The learner is not passive, but the responsibility for learning starts with the
  teacher. ICT is seen as increasing and enhancing the range of possibilities
  for teaching.
- Opening Minds – shifts the curriculum focus from knowledge to capabilities. The emphasis is on skills, the content can be that of the National

Curriculum or something else. ICT is both implicit and explicit in the expected capabilities.

- Enquiring Minds – a similar idea to Opening Minds, only more specifically developing pupils' research skills, and beginning from their personal interests, constructing an interface between formal and informal learning. Involves a shift in teaching and learning approach, and personalising of content. Here ICT is seen as permeating all aspects of pupils' lives and experiences, and its role as a powerful learning tool is acknowledged.
- New Basics – also promotes a skills and capabilities approach to the curriculum, as well as a different approach to content. Here teachers determine the broad headlines of a project and plan the lessons, then work with pupils to formulate aspects of the programme of study. ICT is a core skill, as well as a key tool for delivering the curriculum.
- Personalisation by Pieces – a skills and competence-based programme of study that involves pupils not only as learners, but also as tutors, assessors and mentors. ICT is the sole means of delivery, through the use of personal devices – including PDAs and laptops – and assessment is online.

Accelerated Learning

Developed by Alastair Smith in the mid-1990s, this is an approach to teaching that aims to make learning more engaging and effective.[27] It is based on a four-part cycle: connect, activate, demonstrate, consolidate.

- The aim of the 'Connect' phase is to 'Make learning more personal,' connecting to what has been learned before and what is already known.
- In 'Activation' teachers 'Give the necessary information to begin to solve problems posed,' and 'Give learners the opportunity to construct their own meanings in a variety of group situations.
- With the 'Demonstration' phase the intention is to 'Provide opportunities for learners to 'show they know' through several rehearsals and in multiple modes.
- Finally with 'Consolidation' the pupils 'Reflect on what has been learned and how.' Then 'Preview what will come next lesson.'

(Smith *et al.*, 2003: 20)

While the emphasis is placed on the activities of the teacher, Smith is clear that only the pupil can learn. 'The teacher is introducing and organizing the learning, making it "safe" to try, giving feedback, encouraging, probing with questions and managing the experience throughout. In this role, the teacher is the architect of learning and not the one who delivers cement, sand, water and bricks.' (*Ibid.*: 7)

Accelerated Learning is not a method that is dependent on, or driven by, ICT. But ICT is recognised as a very powerful learning tool with potential to enhance the learning experience for the pupil. 'We embrace new technologies and say that they make an understanding of learning even more important for the teacher. The emerging technologies will not, in themselves, create better learners, but teachers who remain ignorant of their pervasive influence and liberating potential do so at their peril.' (*Ibid.*: 7)

It is the approach to teaching that is innovative, which is then applied to the use of ICT. In the connection phase, for instance, it is suggested that a scrolling PowerPoint presentation is created, to use as a scene-setter as students enter the room, with suitable images and music playing. In activation, they can then create a presentation to showcase their ideas to the class. To demonstrate their learning, they could create an online test or an on-screen concept map, then to consolidate their learning they can use one the teacher has prepared to identify areas where they feel they have gaps in their understanding.

As it can sometimes be problematic to get staff to embrace new technologies when they are first brought into school, Smith suggests that the introduction of Accelerated Learning can be a useful way of getting them accepted – as a powerful teaching device, they enhance the approach. 'ICT should support Accelerated Learning. Here is a valuable peg on which to hang the ICT hat!' (*Ibid.*: 101)

Opening Minds

Opening Minds was first conceived as an innovative approach to the curriculum in 1999 by the RSA.[28] The question it sought to explore was what a curriculum would look like if it were based on competence rather than content. That is, if the intention was to develop skills for learning, rather than to acquire specific, tightly defined knowledge.

Five categories of competence were defined:

- for learning
- for citizenship
- for relating to people
- for managing situations
- for managing information.

Between them these include 24 competences for young people to learn and to demonstrate, focused on the skills and aptitudes needed to form the flexible workforce of the twenty-first century. These are not spread evenly under each heading. 'Competences for managing information', for instance, has only two aspects:

Students would:
- have developed a range of techniques for accessing, evaluating and differentiating information and have learned how to analyse, synthesise and apply it

- understand the importance of reflecting and applying critical judgement, and have learned how to do so.

While this appears to be the area with most direct relevance to ICT, new technologies are not seen as peripheral to the curriculum, but as underpinning it, sometimes explicitly, sometimes implicitly. Under competences for Learning students are expected to 'have achieved high standards of competence in handling information and communications technology and understand the underlying processes'; in Citizenship they are expected to 'understand the social implications of technology'; and within Relating to people they are expected to 'have developed a range of techniques for communicating by different means, and understand how and when to use them'.

Although the curriculum focuses on these competences, which are processes rather than outputs or tangible products, there is still a need for some content to work with. As Dr John Dunford, General Secretary of the Association of School and College Leaders, put it when writing in the *RSA Journal*, 'Competencies cannot be taught in a vacuum. They have to be taught through the content of subjects, although the subjects may be organised in a non-traditional way' (June 2003). The organisation of the content lends itself to more topic-based work that crosses subject boundaries. This is not the only immediate impact that he identifies:

> Analysing the curriculum on the basis of competencies also leads to a stronger focus on the style of teaching and learning. After all, the competence of relating to other people, which includes working in teams, can hardly be absorbed if knowledge is only acquired from a teacher standing at the front of a classroom containing rows of desks. Nor can young people develop their initiative by sitting quietly in receiving mode all the time.
>
> (*Ibid.*)

However, these structural changes to the organisation of the traditional, 'subject silo' timetable do not mean that pupils lose their National Curriculum entitlement. Dr Patrick Hazlewood, head teacher of St John's School and Community College, Marlborough, Wiltshire, writing in the same journal, states that 'Provided that the teaching team has a balance of subject expertise, integration of the National Curriculum should not present a problem.' Three years later, in the February 2006 edition, he went further, talking of ' … a coherent, integrated curriculum that did not recognise subject boundaries and was not limited by the concepts and ideas detailed in the Year 7 National Curriculum.'

Schools that have adopted Opening Minds have found that the shift from a content-driven to a competence-based curriculum produces positive benefits for teaching and learning, with Ofsted considering St John's curriculum 'outstanding'. There was a similar judgement made at Gumley House RC Convent School in Hounslow, London, which found, 'a curriculum which is innovative, responds imaginatively to changing requirements and which promotes high levels of achievement as well as an enjoyment of learning' (Section 5 Inspection, October 2006).

Case study – Integrated learning at Gumley House Convent School

Gumley House RC Convent School is an all-girls Catholic school in Hounslow, south-west London, with around 1200 pupils, including a number of boys in the sixth form. At its last Ofsted inspection in October 2006, it was found to be outstanding.

The school introduced the Opening Minds curriculum three years ago, and it now forms the backbone of the Integrated Learning element of the year seven curriculum. This takes up two days of the timetable, one whole day and two halves each week. Some periods are extended, others are single sessions to fit in with the rest of the school timetable. Integrated Learning takes the place of several traditional subjects, whose programmes of study are met through cross-curricular work, including Drama, Food Technology, Design Technology, PSHE, Citizenship and Geography. There is also an emphasis on developing high-level literacy and numeracy skills, although discrete Maths and English lessons are also on the timetable.

Over the year the girls follow six modules, each lasting half a term. For all of them the year starts with a module on 'Myself', which includes 'I learn' and 'Team learn', to help them get to know themselves as learners, and how to work with others. It also focuses on them growing into adolescence, with lessons on puberty and relationships. The last half-term of the year is taken up with 'Team time', consisting of challenges such as organising a barbecue for the local old people's homes. In between, the programme operates on a carousel basis, with six groups made up of a mixture of the six forms in the year, rotating through four modules. These are: 'News stand'; 'Who wants to be a millionaire?'; 'Story time' and 'Life journeys'. Each has explicit learning objectives both for developing skills as a learner and for curriculum content, with the acronym CLIPS underpinning it all – Citizenship, Learning, Information, People and Situations – the five aspects of Opening Minds. These are distributed across each module, and students are expected to reflect on them as part of their self-evaluation.

In 'Who wants to be a millionaire?', for instance, Citizenship and Learning are expected to be covered through a practical project in the design technology workshop. Here the girls are asked to design a range of novelty chocolates, to make prototype packaging, including the blister wrapping and graphic design, taking into account their target audience. Their teacher, Ken Edwards, believes that Integrated Learning is 'The child of technology, because it is problem solving with a real-life approach.' In his lesson, the pupils sit in groups of four, within which they have to agree their approach to the brief, and each contribute one design for a chocolate novelty and its packaging. Around the room, the time spent on developing skills of cooperation and collaboration are evident.

At one table, four girls, Celine, Megan, Georgia and Katrina, are discussing their ideas for a product. The predominant one is based on popular soft drinks, producing chocolates shaped like miniature cans of top brands. To be sure that all views are heard, they go round the table, taking it in turns to speak and to listen, seeking a consensus. There is a modicum of disagreement from Megan, who is asked to put forward an alternative. When this does not provide a resolution, they decide to move to a vote. At this point, Megan raises her hand and they carry on, pleased that they have got agreement all round. Along the way, each of them has had an opportunity to state an opinion equally, to be sure their voice has been heard, and that the decision arrived at represents all their views. The next decision is what sort of chocolate to use: milk, dark, white, or some of each.

Alongside this, they learned practical workshop skills, such as how to use an electric fretsaw, watched a film about the production of MDF, and found out about the various plastics used for packaging and their environmental impact.

In the other lessons in this module, followed in other parts of the timetable, the elements of Information, People and Situations are covered. The girls will look at different aspects of the commercial world, including working life, such as what it is like to be on the factory floor, and Fair Trade. In the latter area they use the internet to trace the journey of the chocolate, from cocoa-producer to supermarket shelf, accompanied by a breakdown of who earns what along the way. This results in a debate on whether this is a reasonable distribution of the price, and the impact that changes would have on the people along the chain. Members of another class are challenged to use their research to create informative packaging for a Fair Trade café, which needs to be cheap, engaging, and supportive of the concept.

Other modules have similar challenges. In 'Life journeys', pupils use tokens to buy properties in different areas, either rural or urban, and establish a range of services. They have to find solutions to problems, such as housing the homeless; coping with legions of lost pets; finding a solution to an epidemic of dog fleas; or deciding how to respond to a museum that has burnt down, first cleaning up the mess, then deciding whether to replace it, and if so, with what. The tasks draw on the multidisciplinary nature of the teaching team, each contributing ideas that they all help to develop, finalise and draw together.

Given the range of activities and intended learning outcomes involved in Integrated Learning, it is no surprise that the girls give a similarly diverse account of what they have learned. Some, such as Amber, focus on the tangible outputs, the things that they have made, 'learning sewing to make bags' as well as 'books and newspapers'. Chelsey has a broader response: 'We learn loads of different things. We don't do Geography or Food tech. as lessons, so we do them in IL [Integrated Learning]. In 'Who wants to be a millionaire?' we do stuff you used to do in technology.' She also identifies outcomes from the skills elements of the modules: 'They tell you how to learn. How to look after yourself. You do projects on who you were and what you want to achieve. How to achieve more with your work. The teachers tell you about resources that will help you.' In order to illustrate the point, she looks for photographs on the school network that have been used previously in lessons to 'Open up your minds to different ways of seeing things.'

Chelsey is also aware of a different sort of response from the staff: 'Teachers will say "Look at it again" if you get it wrong, rather than say it is wrong.' It is an approach reinforced by Ken Edwards who, in common with other staff, wears a badge on the reverse of the school ID that hangs from his neck asking 'What do you think?' When pupils ask questions that they can resolve for themselves, his response is often 'Talk to the badge.'

For Emma, the main focus of the outcomes of Integrated Learning is much more about personal development and learning to learn. The skills of working in groups, finding information and developing as a learner are the immediate things that come to mind. At the beginning of the year, she discovered she has a preference for kinaesthetic learning, being someone who enjoys physically moving things around – ideas on pieces of paper, perhaps. This focus on her own learning processes has, she believes, helped her to focus. 'Before I had IL I wasn't really concentrating. In "News stand," we got projects to do which helped me to get organised with the timetable and get all my lessons done.' Other benefits have been a better appreciation of different types of text, because, unlike the literacy hour which was 'all about grammar', in 'Story telling' they focus on different ways of telling a story. While this module might have been expected to have echoes of her primary experience, this wasn't the case. Chelsey similarly found that it wasn't like her former school because it was 'How to achieve more with your work.'

This dissimilarity is despite the fact that learning intentions are made quite explicit, as with the Literacy and Numeracy hours in primary schools. In Ken Edwards's lesson, he began by writing up on the board the five tasks making up that day's lesson, and going through what could be achieved individually and which were group tasks. The groups are put together in different ways: sometimes they are self-selected by pupils, but often they are teacher-directed to ensure a balance of skills, and that the girls have to find ways of working together. 'Before, when we were first here, we weren't always talking to each other,' recalls Emma, 'Now we are getting on and talking to each other. We work together.' Working collectively also helps to provide opportunities to 'Do something for the common good,' as Chelsey put it. 'To contribute to a group. You know, you take something out – this lets you put it back.'

In taking greater responsibility for their learning, there is also an impact on behaviour. 'Discipline has to be there,' believes Ken Edwards, 'But they take more responsibility for it themselves, as they do with their learning.'

The experience of following a curriculum with an emphasis on skills and capabilities has been a positive one for staff and pupils alike – even leading to a feeling of having received something others haven't. 'Most of my friends at other schools don't do IL and don't know things we know through doing it,' reports Chelsey. 'It's nice to know you're doing something a bit different from everyone else.'

Enquiring Minds

This originated as a three-year project funded by Microsoft Education in the UK, and carried out by Futurelab, a blue skies technology-in-education research group based in Bristol. Working with two local secondary schools – Ashton Park Community School and Gordano School in Portishead – they sought to explore how students could 'take more responsibility for the content, processes and outcomes of their learning' (Morgan *et al.*, 2007: 4). The starting point was 'that students bring to school valid and important knowledge, and the project is an attempt to bring about deeper engagement in learning by starting from students' own interests and needs'(*Ibid.*)

The reason for wanting to follow this thread is a belief that finding a way of bringing together the structured school curriculum and the learning in which pupils engage outside of school will enable a shift in the education system, to make it more suitable for the twenty-first century.

> The relationship between pedagogy and curriculum, and between 'school' knowledge and students' 'informal' knowledge, is central to the search for more effective and powerful educational strategies for the 21st century. It is these relationships that Enquiring Minds is specifically addressing.
>
> (*Ibid.*: 15)

This project seeks to make learning personal, starting from the student, their interests, their views and beliefs, and aspects of their lives. In order to do this, there also needs to be a shift in the relationship between pupils and staff, from one where teachers have the knowledge and pupils are passive recipients, to one where they become co-creators of it – a social–constructivist approach. The knowledge pupils bring to the lesson is as equally valued as that which the teacher brings. 'The nature of adult/child relationships is shifting. Kids see adults less as authoritative figures and more as co-makers of the learning experience,' believes John Morgan, reporting on the project at 'Why don't you?', a Futurelab conference held in October 2007. In order to do this, he went on to say, 'Teachers have to give up some of the power they have in the classroom.' Which was not the only potentially problematic area they had found. There was also an inclination for schools to create a 'curriculum ghetto', a place where Enquiring Minds became a subject in itself. In particular, it often replaced other subjects concerned with pupils' sense of self or relationships, such as Religious education, PSHE or Citizenship – rather than being seen as a broader approach to learning that permeated the whole timetable.

Given the role that technology plays in young peoples' lives, its ability to support research, and the possibilities for communication, it is unsurprising that ICT has a very important part to play in this approach to the curriculum.

> The idea that information is easily available, and that software enables people to communicate and share information and ideas, has the potential to enable students to participate in knowledge sharing and collaborative production of knowledge both within classrooms and in collaboration with others.
>
> (*Ibid.*: 31)

One example from the handbook (*ibid.*) outlines how communication technologies not only were a means of research, but also provided the focus for study. Students had to focus on ICTs, such as mobile phones or portable games consoles, and make statements about what they meant to them. This was followed up by research to find out how the same devices affected young people globally, connecting a very individual response into a complex, multi-faceted appreciation of how something quite personal affects the world more generally. All of this was structured for them along the way by the class teacher.

Although the implementation of Enquiring Minds in schools has not penetrated as deeply into classroom practice, nor shifted relationships between teaching staff and pupils, as significantly as was hoped, the project has received further funding both to disseminate the findings so far, and to develop further the role of pupils as researchers.

Case study – New basics

Djanogly is a City Academy in Nottingham, which opened in 2003 to replace two schools, its forerunner Djanogly City Technology College (named after its sponsor, Sir Harry Djanogly, a textile magnate) and Forest School. It has a very ICT-rich environment, with one-to-one access to computers in all generic teaching rooms. Corridors have plasma screens at intervals to display work, and the school has a learning platform where pupils are 'only four clicks away from school' – they can log in to their own work and to resources from teachers quickly and easily.

The school recognises that it is not the technology that makes a difference, but the way it is used. Recently, they have introduced into the lower years a curriculum developed in Queensland, Australia, known as New Basics.[29] In this curriculum there are four essential clusters of practice:

- life pathways and social futures
- multi-literacies and communications media
- active citizenship
- environments and technologies.

To demonstrate their learning, pupils then engage in 'Rich Tasks':

A Rich Task is a culminating performance or demonstration or product that is purposeful and models a life role. It presents substantive, real problems to solve and engages learners in forms of pragmatic social action that have real value in the world. The problems require identification, analysis and resolution, and require students to analyse, theorise and engage intellectually with the world. In this way, tasks connect to the world outside the classroom.

(Education Queensland, 2001: 5)

The tasks are intended to be cross-disciplinary, challenging while drawing on different aspects of the clusters, and have a link to the real world outside school. They are introduced through questions and enquiry.

At Djanogly, the introduction of the curriculum into year seven has seen a radical reorganisation of the traditional school structures. The 275 pupils are broken down into four 'pods' of approximately 70. Each is then assigned three teachers from across the staff, ensuring an interdisciplinary approach; an ICT specialist, in recognition of the important role new technologies have in learning at the school; and a teaching assistant. The teaching week nominally has 33 periods, but only the five periods of PE each week are rigidly timetabled, the rest of the time is left for the staff group to arrange as they see fit. In order to do this, the pupils leave at 2:30 on Friday afternoons to give the teaching team two hours of planning time together – in both pod and cross-pod teams.

The school year is broken into five eight-week terms, in the first four of which work is organised with a topic theme, and culminates in a Rich

Task. In the fifth term, they start their year eight work, as the school truncates the Key Stage 3 curriculum into two years so students can start GCSE work a year early.

Thematically, the terms cover 'Science and ethics', 'The built environment', 'Organising and presenting an artistic event' and 'British national identity'. All are cross-curricular. The content of the latter involves History, Geography, questions of philosophy and relationships such as shared values, and activities including the collection and analysis of data. This sees pupils on the streets of the city centre interviewing the public, then compiling the results in order to reach conclusions about what it means to be British.

As they work, students record information electronically and save it to their e-portfolio. Typically, a project will require a mind map to plan, record and structure the learning, developing as the task progresses. The majority of the Rich Tasks will also have a video recording of some aspect, again saved to the e-portfolio to be drawn on as necessary throughout their school career.

The role of ICT is integral to the New Basics curriculum, not because of any particular characteristics it brings to learning, but because new technologies are acknowledged to be embedded within our lives, so capability with them is seen as essential to individual development. Such is the success of the approach that the school is considering extending aspects of it further upwards through the older year groups.

Personalisation by Pieces

This approach begins from the perspective that there are two broad interpretations given to the notion of 'personalisation' in schools. One offers an extension of the tools available to the teacher (the T route), while the other does the same for pupils (the P route).

The first of these sees 'Personalisation as the natural evolution of differentiation', with the teacher having 'more appropriate data and analysis tools for the learners', leading to them make learning more personal. In this mode of thinking, 'the current model of education remains largely intact but is enhanced through ICT and our growing understanding of how learning happens.' (Buckley, 2007: 4)

In the P route, personalisation is seen as 'offering different routes through education for each learner', which extends to breaking free of year groups and the boundaries imposed by subject-based curricula. 'This route would require a transformation of the model of education and would change the current roles of learner and teacher. It would provide greater choice, responsibility and ownership in the hands of learners.' (*Ibid.*)

The Personalisation by Pieces approach is intended to support this P route, but in a scalable way – it can be used as an element of the curriculum, an hour on the timetable through to something that permeates the whole of the school's ethos and educational offering. It argues that the core principles on which the system is based can be extended to a variety of contexts, and is appropriate for all ages and situations, from small children to graduates.

As well as being a lifelong continuum, based on sound research evidence, these core principles include the intention that developments should 'begin with the learner and build up a curriculum from the inside out.' That within this the methods of assessment should be 'owned by the peer group,' and be based on evidence. It should also be 'Able to provide every learner with tangible progress each week.' Finally the curriculum should promote creativity – through activity that is imaginative, purposeful, original and of value in relation to the objective[30] (*ibid.*: 8).

The programme itself is goal-driven, and regular targets are set that are largely determined by the learners themselves, in negotiation with a mentor. To achieve this, the goals have to be understandable by the learner, who has the major responsibility for determining what evidence will be gathered to show that they have been met. The goals themselves will be skills-based, so the content and contexts for working on them can be flexible, perhaps using the National Curriculum or through some other work, such as a personal project, and outputs are agreed with the learner. In this way, while the Personalisation by Pieces programme of study focuses on skills and capabilities, the content through which these are achieved can be drawn from any situation.

The process is that the learner, in conjunction with their mentor – a teacher, parent, another adult in the school, or even someone external – agrees the skills to be learned, the content of that learning, and the evidence to demonstrate that they have been achieved. On completion, this evidence is submitted online to an assessor, ideally a peer who has already achieved two levels ahead on the particular skills ladder. They either agree that the evidence shows the skills have been met, and deposit it in the student's e-portfolio (in some implementations only the assessor can do this), or provide feedback on what else needs to be done to meet the requirements. Once the agreed skills have been mastered, the learner and mentor meet again (usually on a weekly basis) and agree the next set of targets – starting again the cycle of learners setting goals, collecting evidence, self-assessing, submitting, collecting in their e-portfolio, then setting new targets. Once they have progressed at least two stages, they can become involved in assessing others, too.

All of this is structured through skills ladders, 'sets of progressively more challenging problems within a given skill area'. For example, one such skill set is based on the Key Skills framework. It has 20 skill ladders, ranging from 'Researching a problem' to 'Doing calculations' and 'Presenting to an audience', each of which has nine steps to completion. In 'Combining sources' the descriptor for level six is:

> For level 6 you need evidence that you can summarise information. You start with quite large pieces of text and you find all of the main points

then arrange them in order to make your summary. Six or more multiple page sources that you found yourself, summarised to less than a page, should do the trick.

(*Ibid.*: 12).

The use of student-friendly language is very evident here – and is also reflected in the self-assessment questions:

- Did you find at least six sources? (five multiple-page text documents)
- Did you manage to find all of the key points in the sources you found?
- Did you create a one-page summary that had all the main points in a logical order?

(*Ibid.*)

In conventional classroom situations, there may be a tendency for teachers to provide the sources, carefully selected to be at what they consider an appropriate level of challenge for the student, and then possibly a template or writing frame for the summary. This would remove an element of pupil control, so additional criteria may need to be added, such as working on a topic that is new to both pupil and teacher, to ensure the integrity of the task. By providing this level of student ownership, it is suggested that even those who are disengaging from their education can be reconnected.

In our experience it can take up to three years for the culture of children rejecting learning to be overturned. This system achieves this refocus on learning by recognising the learners' view that much of the content they are asked to learn is felt by them to be unnecessary. Rather than repackage this as 'cool', it verifies learning through content recognised by the individual as being of importance.

(Buckley, 2007: 23)

The progression through the skills is recorded in a student profile. This outlines the particular skill ladders the pupil is following, and how far they have progressed on each. By providing this on a handheld device, an outline of the requirements and the agreed evidence can always be readily available, along with contact with the mentor and any assessors, and easy connection to the web for research, communication and collaboration.

The use of peers for assessment utilises characteristics of the web that pupils may well be familiar with from outside school, by posting content for others to view and comment on. It also helps teachers to manage the assessment load, as reviewing and agreeing all the evidence from every pupil could be administratively demanding. Another benefit is that students become reviewers, in itself a very powerful way of reinforcing learning, showing deep understanding of the educational objectives and concepts involved. Built into the system, for quality assurance purposes, is the use of evaluation tools, which means students can give feedback on assessors (rather like the scores given to users of eBay). In order to retain their credibility, those charged with assessment have to maintain their own standards. (Where this system has been evaluated, assessors have been found to be accurate and consistent in their marking and feedback.)

Personalisation by Pieces offers schools a way of introducing radical, transformational change to their ways of working, to a degree they feel comfortable with. The starting point is the personalisation of learning, along a continuum between control by the teacher to control by the pupil. It uses new technologies to enable this to happen. And it gives the option of using existing, structured progressions, through skill sets, or of constructing others more suitable to the students and the context.

If there is an issue that remains to be addressed, it is in shifting public perceptions of the value of such an approach. Existing ways of accrediting learning, predominantly GCSEs and A Levels, are based on learning content, on acquiring knowledge, which is seen as an academic activity. The acquisition of skills tends to be seen as vocational, and therefore of less value. What is needed is a shift to a position where the ability to apply skills and capabilities is seen as valuable, regardless of the subject being studied. This may be helped along the way by the Qualifications and Curriculum Authority's introduction of an 'A' level with open content. That is, without a prescribed course, but focusing on pupils' own research and learning skills, demonstrated through working on a topic of interest to them. The exact format and syllabus for this course have yet to be announced.

Integrated not stand-alone

While all the preceding examples can be introduced as individual initiatives to shift the focus and emphasis of the curriculum, they are not mutually exclusive, and can easily be used together to bring greater personalisation. Opening Minds and Enquiring Minds, for instance, both seek to develop the individual learner's skills: the former has a set of capabilities to shape this learning; the latter is concerned in particular with research skills, developed through using pupils' own interests as a starting point. This can also be the starting point for Personalisation by Pieces, but it needn't be – it is a programme that can easily be implemented using the existing National Curriculum, as can Opening Minds.

The teaching methods propounded by Accelerated Learning would be appropriate to any situation requiring someone to take on that role, including pupils. All the frameworks presented here will require some element of teaching at some point – in many respects they represent a shift in the balance of the relative responsibilities of staff and students.

New Basics proposes to change the curriculum model altogether, removing subject silos and rupturing the boundaries of the timetable. The way staff and pupils work together could accommodate the research skills of Enquiring

Minds, the skills development of Personalisation by Pieces, the focus on learning about learning from Opening Minds, and the pedagogical approaches of Accelerated Learning. All of them contribute to transformation and have a strong component of ICT to underpin them. Whether such approaches will be adopted by schools will be determined by the stage of development a school is at, its ethos and values, and the nature of the relationships between teachers and pupils. And perhaps most critically, by public perceptions of their validity as models of curriculum and learning.

Conclusion

As personalisation continues to permeate schools, so its shape is beginning to take form, supported by a range of professionals and practitioners in an assortment of roles, each contributing to ensuring pupils are given the necessary support to allow effective learning to take place. To help this happen, there are developments within the school that have brought a focus to bear on individual learning needs, creating targets for all.

Alongside this, the constrictions of subject specificity are beginning to break, and a shift from content to skills is taking place. This requires new ways of understanding learning, and ways are emerging that will allow students to demonstrate achievement in new areas and in new ways. Similarly, judgements about schools and their effectiveness are being made with more sophisticated tools against broader criteria, reflecting the changes in desirable outcomes for young people.

While broader systemic change is being introduced through the new National Curriculum, through Building Schools for the Future, and through the inspection regime, other initiatives are demonstrating the possibilities. Change and transformation are achievable – the question is how far do we want to go?

Chapter 5

Can practice meet policy?

The core policies of ensuring Every Child Matters, that their learning is personalised, and that technology is harnessed to ensure these happen are closely interlinked – as are the degrees to which they can achieve their aims. Unless the possibilities of ICT are fully realised, we cannot exploit the opportunities it presents for removing restrictions of time, place, pedagogy and subject choice, which enable and enhance the personalisation agenda. We also need to tap its power to communicate and collaborate in order to identify and support vulnerable children, and to improve the life chances of all our young people.

The degree to which these policies attract support and acceptance varies considerably. For some, the transformational powers of ICT remain unproven, and just what constitutes 'Personalised Learning' remains unclear. And while Every Child Matters is broadly supported, aspects of it, specifically the sharing of information, are, at worst, considered damaging.

There are tensions between systemic demands and personal needs, disputes about the methods by which the desired outcomes are to be achieved, and doubts that little will change except the language we use.

Unproven ICT?

New technologies are expected to support transformational change throughout services for children in a number of ways. As well as connecting professionals and sharing information, the heavy investment in ICT in schools is intended to drive results forward and to provide a structure for personalising learning.

The view that ICT benefits learning almost goes unchallenged. Becta, perhaps understandably, given its role in leading on the role of ICT in education, promotes its effectiveness. A headline from a recent pamphlet for senior managers in schools states categorically: 'Some subject results are known to improve by half a grade when pupils make use of technology to support their learning' (Becta, 2006a).

All well and good – but, given the significant amount of money that has been invested in ICT in recent years, perhaps it is not surprising that Becta should emphasise the positive benefits of that outlay. However, the hint of uncertainty expressed in the use of 'some' is further revealed in other Becta publications that develop this circumspection further.

> The evidence of the impact of ICT on attainment is, as yet, inconsistent, although there are indications that in some contexts, with some pupils, in some disciplines, attainment has been enhanced. There is not a sufficient body of evidence in any of these areas, however, to draw firm conclusions in terms of explanatory or contributory factors.
>
> (Condie *et al.*, 2007: 29)

There are some studies, conducted independently of Becta, that go further in questioning its conclusions, leading to suggestions that the investment in ICT could have been better spent in other ways. One study has found that while investment in computers raises attainment, investment in books has a greater impact.

> They [the researchers] have come to the conclusion that spending £100 per pupil on books has a greater impact on average test scores across English, Maths and Science than the same amount spent on ICT or staffing.
>
> They found the average Key Stage 2 test score was 27.5 and estimated that schools which spent £100 per pupil on books raised test scores from an average 27.5 to 27.9, or 1.5 per cent per child. This compared to £100 on ICT, which would raise scores by 0.72 per cent per child.
>
> (Ward, 2006)[1]

Going further than this in finding that new approaches are not as effective as previous ones, is an international study from Germany suggesting that not only does technology not enhance learning, it actually has a retrograde effect. Fuchs and Woessmann (2004) came to a number of conclusions. They looked at the availability of computers in the home, and took into account other factors that may be present, other than the machines. 'We show that the statistically significant positive correlation between the availability of computers at home and student performance in math and reading reverses into a statistically significantly negative one as soon as other family-background influences are extensively controlled for in multivariate regressions.' They go on to draw a similar conclusion around access to ICT in schools, 'because the availability of school computers is strongly correlated with the availability of other school resources.' (*Ibid.*: 1). However, availability is not the only issue – it also depends what the computers are used for.

> Third, we show that the relationship between computers and student learning differs strongly between the mere availability of computers and their use as a communicational and educational device. At home, the negative relationship of student performance with computer availability contrasts with positive relationships with the use of computers for emailing,

webpage access and the use of educational software. Thus, the mere availability of computers at home seems to distract students from learning, presumably mainly serving as devices for playing computer games. Only by using computers in constructive ways can the negative effect of computer provision on student learning be partly compensated for.

(*Ibid.*: 2)

This finding seems to be reinforced by their final conclusion that 'students who never use computers or the internet at school show lower performance than students who sometimes use computers or the internet at school. But students who use them several times a week perform even lower. ... the pattern might suggest that there is an optimal level of computer and internet use at school, substantially below a use intensity of several times a week.' (*Ibid.*)

An appropriate response to the findings of this international survey is that we not only need to regulate and control the amount of access pupils have to new technologies, but also to seek an optimum level of use. Fuchs and Woessmann do not speculate on what this might be – how many hours per week, on what activities, and whether age differentials need to be taken into account. Condie *et al.* (2007), focusing on the use of ICT in England, agree, at least in part: 'The availability of ICT is not, in itself, sufficient to enhance learning and teaching and, in turn, increase attainment' (*ibid.*: 63). But they differ from their German colleagues in their reservations about its use in the classroom: 'Where ICT has become a regular part of the classroom experience, there is evidence of positive impact on learning and pupil performance' (*ibid.*: 23). They also point out that 'the evidence seems to point to an impact on attainment where ICT is an integral part of the day-to-day learning experiences of pupils, although the weight of evidence is insufficient to draw firm conclusions' (*ibid.*: 24).

Despite the difficulties of trying to determine just what difference ICT makes to pupils' learning and therefore attainment, and how and why this might happen, the argument about whether to continue the degree of investment to which the current government has committed appears to have been decided – it will continue. According to research by Kable, part of the Guardian News & Media Group:

ICT is playing an increasingly important role in the delivery of learning and teaching. Underlying technology is improving communications and the management of information. Year on year expenditure growth in education ICT, estimated at 4.6%, is higher than the total education expenditure growth of 4%. ICT will be worth £2.9bn by 2009/10 – an increase of more than £470m from 2005/6.[2]

There may be sound reasons for this continuing high level of investment. One study, approaching the question of the link between attainment and expenditure from an economic perspective, found a direct link in some respects. The work, based on changes in government funding to schools in the first few years of this decade, found that large-scale investments could make a difference.

> In contrast with most previous studies in the economic literature, we find evidence for a positive impact of ICT investment on educational performance in primary schools. A positive effect is observed for English and Science, though not for Mathematics. Hence it seems that, in a context where there was a significant expansion of ICT investment, one can uncover evidence of an improvement in pupil achievement linked to ICT.
>
> (Machin et al., 2006: 21)

Although ICT has been in use in UK schools for at least three decades, there may be an argument that it is still too early to determine what impact it has had – or even that the discussion about past and future investment is not fruitful, that the picture in schools has changed, and that new technologies will increasingly become integral to them. It seems that scepticism about new trends in education is not a new phenomenon.

> Computing technologies have been heavily criticised by educationalists and educational philosophers as a vehicle to promote shallow learning, mindless copying and pasting, and decontextualised acquisition of definitions and facts. In short, a tool for 'jogging the memory, not for remembering … [providing students] with the appearance of intelligence, not real intelligence … they will seem to [have] wide knowledge, when they will usually be ignorant … '.
>
> The quotation above however, is not from a modern educationalist, mistrustful of new technology, but is adapted from Plato's *Phaedrus* … in which the author recalls Socrates' criticisms of writing.
>
> (Madden et al., 2005: 3)

There are several issues that can be raised with research into the use of ICT in schools, amongst them that they are measuring the impact of the new technologies against outcomes relevant to education before their introduction. That amongst the changes that ICT may bring about are ways of learning, demonstrating achievement and personal development that were not previously possible.

> 'Sure they have short attention spans – for the old ways of learning,' says a professor.[3] Their attention spans are not short for games, for example, or anything else that actually interests them. As a result of their experiences Digital Natives crave interactivity – an immediate response to their each and every action. Traditional schooling provides very little of this

compared to the rest of their world (one study showed that students in class get to ask a question every 10 hours). So it generally isn't that Digital Natives can't pay attention, it's that they choose not to.

(Prensky, 2001: 4)

This is not to say that Prensky believes changes to the ways in which children and young people behave when working are all positive. 'One key area that appears to have been affected is reflection. ... .In our twitch-speed world, there is less and less time and opportunity for reflection, and this development concerns many people' (*ibid.*: 5).

Not only are our behaviours and ways of thinking changing, but we also need to find new measurements for the impact of ICT because it is emerging through outputs that have not been available before. The skill of remembering facts may give way to that of finding them, reflecting and analysing them, and assessing their value for the task in hand. Text literacy remains important, but what about visual literacy? We will always need to know how to do calculations, but creating a formula so the machine can do the job, then interpreting the outputs, may be more valuable.

Unfortunately this extraordinary potential for progress comes at a time when we are wedded to an assessment model that satisfies us if children attempt the same activities as their predecessors, but do so a little better. In an age of rapid progress this fatally masks rapidly falling standards and stultifies ambition. On the one hand new technology supports children's ability to make new leaps of imagination and creativity, yet a reliance on criterion referencing denies the value of that imagination and creativity by excluding it under the feeble pretext that it wasn't how we did it before. The result is that schools habitually confiscate or deny new technology removing everything from ball-point pens ('it will spoil your handwriting') to mobile phones ('disruptive') and teachers report that the best creativity they observe is in the non-curriculum space of lunchtime clubs or out of school activities. We have failed to respond within the curriculum and its assessment process to these new opportunities for creativity.[4]

We have ways of thinking and working that are embedded in the education system. New technologies are providing a challenge to these, but there is a reluctance to embrace them fully and allow change to happen. This has led Selwyn and Young (2007) to note that:

...the integration of IT into schools to date has been inconsistent, with schools appearing to prove remarkably 'resistant' to technological change. This has led some authors to observe that technology is constantly fighting a battle against pre-existing educational culture, occasionally succeeding but generally failing to be effectively adopted.

Maybe this reluctance to embrace technological change is, in part, because education is a system that we have all passed through, that we all have our own, particular, understanding of, and so it presents a personal challenge to accept it into our conceptions of schooling. ICTs are presenting us with new possibilities, new routes through learning, that are largely untravelled. We are concerned for the futures of those who would be the pioneers.

Are the engines of change strong enough to break the bonds of the system?

The pace of change may be inhibited by our system's deeply rooted development. Orthodoxies have arisen that it is difficult to counter. These can be seen to have come about to satisfy systemic rather than personal needs. The challenge currently is to shift that balance, to bring the personal to the forefront – although it can be argued that this approach will lead to fragmentation by trying to meet too many individual goals, that the education system is designed for the good of society, and it is the collective needs, therefore, that it should satisfy.

Many aspects of the development of the education system in this country can be understood as one of its changing to meet the needs of various interest groups and national imperatives, rather than the needs of the individuals going through it.

- The school year, with its longer breaks at Easter and summer, is there to meet the needs of agriculture, first sowing and then reaping.
- Compulsory education came about to both release adults to work in the factories, and to provide the more educated labour force that advances in production methods and commerce required.
- Exams were originally developed to provide a filter for those wishing to enter the Civil Service.
- School meals were introduced because of the poor physical condition of military recruits.
- The school-leaving age has been gradually rising to improve skills levels for future employment; and to the lower the number of people in the workforce, and therefore the numbers of unemployed declared in government statistics.
- Break times were introduced to air classrooms following their occupation by hosts of unwashed children and the open fires that warmed them, rather than as an opportunity for play and socialisation.

As for the curriculum, since its inception it has been shifting to meet the needs, variously, of the Empire, commerce, and industry, with schools tiered to provide the managerial, technical and labouring workforces. What attempts there have been to shift to more child-centred education, as suggested for instance by the Plowden Report in the 1960s, have been largely vilified by the press for their soft, liberal philosophies. Universal, comprehensive education has never been achieved, and the introduction of academies and specialist secondary schools by the current government has echoes of the former tripartite system, which lives on in the grammar and technical schools scattered around the country.

It is also a system that can be thought of as being deliberately impersonal, demoting individuality and promoting uniformity. Pupils are largely required to look the same and act the same, to learn the same things at the same times, sitting in uniform rows, in an appropriate posture, listening attentively. The terms of address generally used seem to be designed to maintain a distance between pupils and staff, and to emphasise the balance of power in the relationship, using the familiarity of forenames for pupils and the deferential mode of surnames for staff. Yet pupils often learn best from those with whom they feel a personal connection, rather than a deliberate disconnection.

Then there are the strictures of time and place. In the UK, formal education begins at five years old, whereas for many of our European neighbours the curriculum lacks a noticeable structure until pupils reach seven. Stating that there is a chronological point at which children become ready to learn formally denies their individuality, as though they are raw material ready for the machine.

The conclusion of compulsory education – currently the end of the summer term of the school year in which a student reaches 16 – seems similarly concerned with the need to move them out of the system, rather than that their individual, personal learning goals are met. What meaning would compulsory education have if pupils really did take control of their own learning, and could choose when it began and ended? While that may be a distant event, much more imminent is the need to address the concept of attendance. Potentially, ICT can allow learning to take place at any time or place, so does there still need to be a requirement for them to arrive, punctually, in their form room?

> A further complication is that the focus on attendance requirements doesn't sit easily with the rationale of distance learning, and e-learning initiatives have even begun to blur the distinction between physical classroom presence and what might be called 'e-presence', seen as another active form of engagement between teachers and pupils.
>
> (Marks, 2006: 9)

While 'personalisation' is seen as having specific elements, degrees of which can potentially be delivered within existing structures, ICT can allow for more personal choice. Some pupils may want to start learning earlier in the day than others, and some will want to work into the small hours of the night. There are those who may want to finish one task before beginning another, and those who prefer to have several projects to switch between at any one time. Alongside time management, there are issues of the choice of subject, the mode of delivery, and the tutor leading the learning.

There are times, it could be argued, when the current system allows greater opportunities for the individual to choose what they want to learn, most noticeably at the extreme ends of the education timeline. In nursery classes, teachers put out a number of areas to attract children's interest, such as water play, a sandpit, the home corner, and so on, then engage and interact depending on what the child does. It is child-led, but teaching staff will look to extend their understanding, and often guide them to try something else. At university, graduates can select their own PhD topics – taking into account factors such as available funding and future employment prospects – guided by their tutor. Again, they will be supported throughout their studies with tasks and tutorials. The task is to provide similar degrees of pupil choice to bridge the gap between the two.

How deep are the roots of Personalised Learning?

The move towards introducing Personalised Learning in schools seems to have arrived suddenly. It was first mentioned by (then) Prime Minister Tony Blair in his Labour Party Conference speech in September 2003. The concept was then fleshed out with a ministerial speech by David Miliband to the North of England Education Conference in January 2004. It did not emerge from methodical research or well considered enquiry, like such forerunners as 'child-centred' education did with the Plowden Report in the late 1960s. Some of the confusion around what constitutes Personalised Learning is due to its provenance.

> It has not been generated by a line of academic research, by practitioners explaining new practice – although it has been picked up and used by some – or through a programme of policy development. In that sense, the task is to understand what is in the mind of ministers, and to work out how their new thinking can be applied on the ground. ... It must be said here that the prior question for some in the education community, and not only those classroom infantry often considered unduly cynical, is whether 'personalised learning' has any real meaning at all.
>
> (Johnson, 2004: 4)

Despite the lack of clarity about just what 'Personalised Learning' is, the term has been embraced and adopted by the education system with a degree of certainty and confidence that belies any such doubts.

> We learn that while 'The school of the future must have personalised learning as its starting point' (Stewart, 2004), engagement with practitioners,

academics and policy-makers (Johnson, 2004) revealed two things: firstly, that 'There was a consensus that there was a lot of confusion out there about what personalised learning meant' and, secondly, that 'despite the lack of clarity, the phrase is spreading like a virus through the system, with schools advertising for teachers with experience and understanding of personalised learning' (Stewart, 2004).

(Fielding, 2006: 348)

Regardless of this lack of definition, Fielding believes the concept could be seen as one that 'at first glance and on first hearing seems to have within it a much needed return to concerns for the wider, human purposes of schooling that give education its enduring significance and satisfaction' (*ibid.*). However, given the lack of certainty about what the concept is, he believes the term 'personalised learning' lends itself to 'performativity' – a focus on performance and outputs that is 'diminishing of our humanity, it is, as many of us have for many years been at pains to point out, unlikely to produce the kinds of results it anticipates and requires. Transformation, not improvement, is to be the order of the day and knowledge creation and networking, not central control, are to be the key agents of its realization' (*ibid.*: 347)

The suggestion is that the personalisation agenda risks placing a greater emphasis on the formal achievement of individuals, which in turn gets in the way of us recognising their broader development, rather than their outputs. This also inhibits the role of schools as a means of ensuring the wider mores of society are understood and distributed.

The Government must also recognise the negative impact of a further stress on individual academic attainment as the purpose of schools. There is always a need to balance this against the social purposes of schools, in terms both of pupils learning social skills and also of their wider aims such as the inculcation of values and the promotion of social cohesion. Talk of personalised learning increases the perception of schooling as a commodity, but centre-left governments should stress its vital contribution to society as a whole.

(Johnson, 2004: 17)

Johnson puts this in the context of the policies of a Labour government as 'The role of governments of the left and centre-left is to emphasise and support the collective in social life as a balance against the individualistic.' He sees personalisation as promoting, as commodifying, learning and achievement, underplaying 'the importance of schools as binding constituents of society, as agents for stability, security, and collective consciousness. The more schools are described as agents of individual academic success, the less they will be perceived as community assets. The more schools are encouraged to develop unique selling points, the less they will be minded to meet the needs of all local children' (*ibid.*: 16).

Neither Johnson nor Fielding is opposed to a shift to a curriculum that is more sensitive to the needs of each individual and conducive to promoting their development holistically. They are concerned that the focus on individual outcomes, in some possible manifestations of its implementation, could place undue emphasis on personal achievement and its being targeted to meet the goal-driven needs of the institution, rather than the personal needs of the pupil. Fielding believes this could manifest itself as a 'new totalitarianism'.

> In its most advanced manifestation personalization is set to become the forerunner of 21st century totalitarianism, promising individual atten-tiveness and fulfilment at the cost of the very self it seems to so ardently celebrate. This does not have to be so. Personalization not only has within it the capacity to counter much that is unjust, unkind and per-nicious in our formal education system, it also has the capacity to explore and develop forms of engagement and ways of learning that contribute to a wider and deeper human flourishing than the present currently affords us. What I have argued for in this paper is an approach that takes a considered, explicit view of what it is to be and become a person.
>
> (Fielding, 2006: 366)

This tension between the need of institutions to be accountable through tangible, measurable outcomes, and the desire to ensure each individual learns in a way that is most beneficial to them, and that retains and develops their interests, is what will determine the degree to which there is a shift in teaching and learning in schools. A move from a system organised around practical considerations of space, time and personnel, to one where the resources are organised for the benefit of the students – not the students for the benefit of the resources. As Futurelab describes it:

> personalisation: Personalised learning is an approach which advocates reversing the logic of education systems so that the system conforms to the learner, rather than the learner to the system, offering bespoke support for each individual in order to foster engaged and independent learners able to reach their full potential.
>
> (www.futurelab.org.uk/glossary)

While this may not entirely conform either to the view given by David Miliband when he first outlined the policy in 2004, or that of the Gilbert Review when it reported in 2006 (see Chapter One), it does encapsulate the transformation necessary to create an education system where personalisation becomes a concept that we can all readily understand.

Can every child matter?

The Every Child Matters agenda differs markedly from that of 'Personalised Learning' in that it has a discernible pedigree. While it overtly emerged through the Children Act 2004 arising from the Laming Report, most of the provisions were already being considered for implementation, and were given an added impetus by the death of Victoria Climbié.

While the proposed intentions of the policy, to improve life outcomes for all children, are generally accepted, one aspect in particular has raised considerable debate – that of the sharing of information about children and young people considered to be vulnerable in some way. This is because of doubts not that doing so will have beneficial effects, but that the blanket nature of the approach is unnecessary, and that the resources given over to it could be better used to support those who have been identified and for whom an intervention is being provided.

The Foundation for Information Policy Research, summarising a report into children's databases published by the Information Commissioner, lists five concerns regarding the policy.[5] The first is that the strategy will 'divert resources and attention away from frontline services'. They cite a figure of 50,000 children at serious risk of harm of whom agencies are aware – extending the range of children and young people reported on to 3 or 4 million could, they believe, divert resources from those who need them most.

Secondly, they believe systems designed to identify and highlight those who are vulnerable may lead to them being labelled in some way, which will have an impact on how they are perceived by those in authority. Teachers may have lower expectations of them, or police officers may treat them as perpetrators, rather than victims or witnesses.

The Foundation for Information Policy Research also supports the belief that closer monitoring of children will remove responsibility from parents for ensuring their offspring are developing properly. Greater involvement of professionals and practitioners will result in 'micromanaged targets for every child, with responsibility for achieving them placed on children's services, rather than parents.'

There are also concerns about children providing data about themselves and agreeing to its being shared, even being 'bullied' into it, and that families' privacy and autonomy will be 'corroded'. Authorities may intervene without providing families with a choice about whether they receive help, or the nature of the support given.

The Foundation quotes Dr Eileen Munro of the London School of Economics as saying 'When dealing with child abuse, we do need to override privacy. But the new policy extends this level of intrusion into families that are not even suspected of abusing their children, and to all concerns about children's development. It will also over-stretch scarce resources, damage parents' confidence and divert services from focusing on real cases of abuse.'

Beyond these concerns are those, unrealised as yet because of the delay in implementation, regarding the ability of practitioners to deal with the information that becomes available, both coping with the possible volume and assessing and analysing it. In addition there is the question of practical operation of the online system, which may challenge the computer skills of some practitioners.

In the grand tradition of government ICT procurement, ContactPoint will not be implemented until several months after its original start-up date, in part due to concerns about data security that have been raised since several high-profile incidents have hit the headlines. The DCSF has commissioned the management consultants Deloitte to assess the security of the system. They point out that:

> It should be noted that risk can only be managed, not eliminated, and therefore there will always be a risk of data security incidents occurring. What is important is that all practical steps to reduce the risk of incidents occurring are taken and when an incident occurs, that it is handled and managed effectively.
>
> (DCSF, 2008b: 4)

They also take into account the human factor, stating that 'While the ContactPoint team can design strong controls into the system and provide good advice to connecting organisations, there is a limit to their ability to enforce good practice or to monitor incidents and control breakdowns' (*ibid.*: 5). However, they stop short of calling for the database to be cancelled, seeming to accept that as far as possible the levels of risk are manageable and acceptable, and are being dealt with appropriately.

One aspect of putting the Every Child Matters policy into practice that has not been scrutinised so closely, or criticised so vehemently, has been the growth of extended schools. As a whole, these received a glowing report from Ofsted, who found that

> The majority of children, young people and their families stated that the main benefits of the services were enhanced self-confidence and improved relationships. Children and adults had heightened aspirations and developed more positive attitudes to learning.
>
> (Ofsted, 2006a: 5)

Ofsted also found that 'The services had a strong influence on participants' health and safety. Enjoyment was an integral part of provision' (*ibid.*), as well as that they had positive impacts on learning, and many of them used 'electronic monitoring systems' to help measure and track the outcomes of families' engagement with them.

Changes to schools therefore appear to be achieving the aims of at least one aspect of the policy themes running through this book. By broadening the services available, they are meeting the wider aims of the five outcomes, not just that of 'enjoying and achieving' embedded in the formal curriculum. A question that remains is: why has the policy come into being in the first place? – beyond a response to the need to protect children, to stop dreadful things happening to them. One perception, from Futurelab, is that it is a response to the changing nature of childhood.

> It is important that all schools provide opportunities for children to thrive. However, the answer to the question of why every child matters is far from clear-cut. Is it in order to fulfil their economic potential and add to the nation's stock of human capital? Is it to ensure that all children are able to live and participate in communities that are safe, harmonious and culturally diverse? Or is it to allow all children to 'find their level' in a society that allocates economic rewards according to success in examinations? The answer as to why every child matters may be all of these and more. Viewed in a wider perspective (and in the British context at least), the drive to ensure that every child matters is to result in [the biggest] transformations in the experience of childhood since the Second World War. Changes in family structure, growing concerns about the risks of childhood, along with the emergence of digital cultures based around the computer screen, mobile phone and text-messaging have led to new forms of childhood. How schools, and society as a whole, respond to these changes is of paramount importance.
>
> (Futurelab, 2008)

The ways in which schools, and society as a whole, respond to current changes provide the key to success – and not just in the Every Child Matters area of policy. The challenge of implementing Personalised Learning will see how far the bounds of the education system can be stretched – perhaps to breaking point – in order to bring about a system that meets individual and societal needs for the twenty-first century. Many of these shifts in education, and in wider children's services, depend on how ready we are to embrace new technologies and harness them to the engine of change.

Notes

1 Policy development and interconnection

1 Projected from 1997–2002, in ONS (1998).
2 Becta stands for British Educational Communications and Technology Agency, see www.becta.org.uk
3 So called after the 1985 legal challenge to doctors' rights to provide contraception to girls beneath the age of consent.
4 For more information see the Help section of www.satsguide.co.uk
5 This is based on solution-focused brief therapy approaches, and can be used online or as a stand-alone application. See www.waysforward.com
6 For more information see www.textsomeone.com
7 For more information visit www.accipio-learning.com
8 See www.truancycall.com
9 Visit www.ratemyteachers.com

2 What can the technology do for us?

1 See http://docs.google.com for more on this facility.
2 See www.redhalo.com
3 See www.youtube.co.uk
4 Flickr, at www.flickr.com, is only one example of a photo-sharing site; others include Picasa from Google: http://picasa.google.com
5 Sign up for a blog at www.blogger.com
6 First Class (www.firstclass.com) and Blackboard (www.blackboard.com) are frameworks for online learning used mainly in higher education.
7 Moodle is also a framework for creating online learning modules. It is open source so bears no cost – except for hosting and local support (http://moodle.org).
8 See www.blizzard.com/us/press/080122.html
9 See www.runescape.com
10 See www.clubpenguin.com
11 See www.habbo.com
12 For a final evaluation of the project see www.flatprojects.org.uk/projects/b_north-easteduc/globalclassroom.asp
13 Cyberlink is developed by Brain Activated Technologies. More information can be found at www.brainfingers.com
14 Prensky is quoting John T. Bruer (1999) *The Myth of the First Three Years*, The Free Press, New York, p. 155.

15 Prensky is quoting Frank D. Roylance (2000) 'Intensive Teaching Changes Brain', Sunspot, Maryland Online Community, 27 May.

16 From *Time*, 5 July 1999.

17 Behaviourism is associated with psychologists such as B. F. Skinner. For more information see Rachlin (undated).

18 This is a product of Widgit software, www.widgit.com

19 For more see www.cricksoft.com

20 See www.frankwise.oxon.sch.uk

21 See www.facebook.com

22 See www.myspace.com

23 See www.friendsreunited.co.uk

24 See www.linkedin.com

25 See www.secondlife.com

26 www.sandaigprimary.co.uk

27 hopeblog.ethink.org.uk

28 Becta is the government agency responsible for developing the use of ICT in education, and therefore for delivering the e-learning strategy embodied in Harnessing Technology. See www.becta.org.uk for more information.

29 Futurelab is a charity engaged in research into innovative uses of ICT in education: www.futurelab.org.uk

30 Buzz is developed for the Sony Playstation. See uk.playstation.com for more information.

31 Altered Learning originated at North West Notts College in Mansfield (www.alteredlearning.com), and modified Never Winter Nights, originally published by Atari (www.atari.com).

32 DoomEd is a modification of Half Life Two by DESQ Ltd. See www.desq.co.uk/doomed for details.

33 See www.dimensionm.com

34 More about Immersive Education can be found at www.immersiveeducation.com

35 Scratch can be downloaded from http://scratch.mit.edu

36 Thinking Worlds from Caspian Learning can be found at www.thinkingworlds.com

37 Visit www.africam.com for live webcams of African wildlife.

38 Available from www.rm.com

39 Available from www.dyslexic.com/audio-notetaker. It also presents audio files on screen as strings of coloured blocks, each representing a word, for easier editing of sound recorded notes.

40 From www.bbc.co.uk/schools/gcsebitesize/mobile

41 Available in the UK from www.valiant-technology.com

42 Download Read in Microsoft Reader from www.microsoft.com/reader/developers/downloads/rmr.mspx

43 Visit www.wildknowledge.co.uk for more details.

44 A free download available from www.mscapers.com

45 Eduinnova and Synchroneyes are distributed in the UK by Steljes. See www.steljes.co.uk for more information.

46 Some of these comments were included in a *Guardian* Link article on 6 May 2008: www.guardian.co.uk/education/2008/may/06/link.news1

47 Becta developed a specification for what a learning platform should be able to do, and offered providers the opportunity to have their products measured against it. Ten companies that met the requirements are included on an approved suppliers list. See http://localauthorities.becta.org.uk – Personalised learning, Learning platforms.

48 See www.learning-styles-online.com/inventory

49 Visit www.infed.org/thinkers/gardner.htm#multiple_intelligences for information on the criteria for being considered discrete intelligence.

50 For an example see www.acceleratedlearning.com/method/test_launch.html
51 From the National Foundation for Educational Research; see www.gl-assessment. co.uk for a range of tests and screeners available.
52 From Lucid Research – see www.lucid-research.com
53 See www.solutionsfinding.com for more information.
54 See www.waysforward.com
55 Visit www.rm.com/Secondary
56 See www.truancycall.com
57 www.capitaes.co.uk
58 More information about this information-sharing database is available at www. everychildmatters.gov.uk/deliveringservices/contactpoint

3 A web of support

1 For more on ContactPoint see the Every Child Matters briefing sheet at www. everychildmatters.gov.uk/_files/B5E2EE3DBBB7E338AB05B1B7D3F5F33A.pdf
2 For ARCH's views on ContactPoint see www.youtube.com and search for contact-point.
3 To download the CAF referral form visit www.everychildmatters.gov.uk/resources-and-practice/TP00004
4 Gillick competence arises from a court case in the mid-1980s when a court permitted medical services to provide birth control to a young person without the parents' knowledge. While it has not been tested in the courts beyond the Health Service, it is taken to be that a young person can take responsibility for giving their own consent as long as a professional believes that the young person understands fully what is being asked of them.
5 More information can be found at www.esprit-is.com
6 To download the Tower Hamlets e-CAF form, visit www.lgfl.net/lgfl/leas/tower-hamlets/accounts/THe%20Grid/everychildmatters/web/CAF/CAF%20Forms/?verb= list where notes to support its completion can also be found.
7 Such approaches have their origins in solution-focused brief therapy. Originating in California, this is based on the fact that most people visit a therapist on only one occasion, so to maximise the time it is best to focus on the future rather than revisit problems from the past. Strengths and resources are found within the individual and progress is sought in small steps, moving gradually up a scale.
8 See http://forensicsoftware.co.uk for more on Policy Central.
9 A charity started by Mike Fischer, one of the original founders of Research Machines; see www.fischertrust.org for more information.
10 For the list of approved suppliers visit http://localauthorities.becta.org.uk – Procurement – Learning platforms.
11 See www.accipio-learning.co.uk and www.nisai.com
12 See www.vision2learnforschools.com for information about the range of courses.
13 From the home page of the charity at www.notschool.net/inclusiontrust.org/ Welcome.html
14 See www.firstclass.com
15 See case studies at www.notschool.net/inclusiontrust.org/IT-media-casestudies.html
16 This list is available to local schools and also to neighbouring authorities; both can purchase from it with confidence, as companies must meet the requirements of the specification to be included on the list.
17 See www.thewhocarestrust.org.uk and the associated site www.whocaresxtra.org. uk, an online magazine with content appropriate for children and young people in public care, including guidance on rights and a problem page.

18 See www.tactcare.org.uk

19 The project has been evaluated from the beginning by Sheffield University Department of Education. See www.shef.ac.uk/inclusive-education/researchwork/projects to download the latest outcomes.

20 See www.chrysalis-club2000.org.uk

21 See www.asdan.co.uk

4   A web for learning

1 These are listed with further detail at www.standards.dfes.gov.uk/personalisedlearning/five

2 For more on Club Tech in the USA visit www.microsoft.com/about/corporatecitizenship/citizenship/giving/programs/up/casestudies/clubtech.mspx

3 See www.iepwriter.com

4 See www.onestopeducation.co.uk

5 See www.capitaes.co.uk/sims

6 For a detailed explanation of how the calculations are carried out download the guidance from www.dcsf.gov.uk/performancetables/schools_06/s12.shtml

7 See http://documents.google.com to collaborate online on working documents.

8 See www.j2e.com to try this out.

9 Visit http://vital.cs.ohiou.edu/vitalwiki/index.php/Second_Life_Development to see the range of projects developed here.

10 www.skoolaborate.com for more details including all the objectives.

11 See http://creators.xna.com

12 These courses can be found at http://msdn2.microsoft.com/en-us/beginner/bb308754.aspx [accessed 20 April 2008].

13 For more information and to download the program visit http://education.mit.edu/starlogo

14 To see a gallery of examples and to download the program go to http://scratch.mit.edu

15 Papert worked in a number of fields, principally mathematics education and artificial intelligence. Visit his website – www.papert.org – for information on his current activities.

16 Visit www.microworlds.com for more.

17 For the full report see http://image.guardian.co.uk/sys-files/Education/documents/2002/12/03/alevelinquiry.pdf

18 See http://dida.edexcel.org.uk/home

19 See www.immersiveeducation.com

20 See www.imedia.ocr.org.uk/centres/intro.htm

21 For more information visit www.bcs.org/server.php?show=nav.8945

22 To download the full report, or the executive summary, visit www.dfes.gov.uk/byronreview

23 Leitch (2006), see www.hm-treasury.gov.uk/independent_reviews/leitch_review/review_leitch_index.cfm

24 From http://curriculum.qca.org.uk/key-stages-3-and-4/developing-your-curriculum/new_opportunities/index.aspx

25 From http://curriculum.qca.org.uk/key-stages-3-and-4/aims/index.aspx

26 For full details of the programme see www.standards.dfes.gov.uk/sie/eic

27 The Accelerated Learning website has more information: www.alite.co.uk

28 See www.thersa.org/projects/education/opening-minds

29 Visit http://education.qld.gov.au/corporate/newbasics

30 Taken from the National Advisory Committee on Creative and Cultural Education's four characteristics of creative processes.

5   Can policy meet practice?

1 Helen Ward's article in the *Times Educational Supplement* is on a research paper entitled 'Has the Literacy Hour reduced reading and book use in primary schools?' by Hurd, S., Dixon, M. and Oldham, H., presented to the British Education Research Conference, 2006.

2 See   www.kable.co.uk/kabledirect/index.php?option=com_content&task=view& id=335731

3 Prensky is quoting Dr Edward Westhead, Professor of Biochemistry (retired), University of Massachusetts.

4 From the weblog of Professor Stephen Heppell, formerly Director of Ultralab, www.heppell.net/weblog/stephen/2007/01/29/Assessmentandnewtechnologyne.html

5 'IT systems designed to protect kids will put them at risk instead', www.fipr.org/press/061122kids.html

Bibliography

Abbott, C. (2007) *E-inclusion: Learning Difficulties and Digital Technologies*, Futurelab, Bristol.

Alloway, T.P. (2007) *Automated Working Memory Assessment (AWMA)*, Pearson Assessment, London.

ARCH (undated) 'Children's databases', Action on Rights for Children, London, www.arch-ed.org/issues/databases/databases.htm

Arnold, T., Cayley, S. and Griffith, M. (2002) *Video Conferencing in the Classroom*, Devon County Council, Exeter.

Audit Commission (2002) *Special Educational Needs: A Mainstream Issue*, Audit Commission, London.

Bayliss, V. (2003) *Opening Minds, Taking Stock*, Royal Society for the Encouragement of Arts, Manufactures and Commerce (RSA), London.

Becta (2002) *ImpaCT2: The Impact of Information and Communication Technologies on Pupil Learning and Attainment*, British Educational Communications and Technology Agency, Coventry.

—— (2003) *What the Research Says about Video Conferencing in Teaching and Learning*, British Educational Communications and Technology Agency, Coventry.

—— (2004) *Evaluation of the DfES Video Conferencing in the Classroom Project*, University of Leicester School of Education/University of Cambridge for the British Educational Communications and Technology Agency, Coventry.

—— (2005) *Extending the Boundaries of Learning*, British Educational Communications and Technology Agency, Coventry.

—— (2006a) *Making a Difference with Technology for Learning: Evidence for School Leaders*, British Educational Communications and Technology Agency, Coventry.

—— (2006b) *Learning Platform Functional Requirements, Version 1*, British Educational Communications and Technology Agency, Coventry.

—— (2006c) *Learning Styles – An Introduction to the Research Literature*, British Educational Communications and Technology Agency, Coventry.

—— (2007a) *Impact Study of e-portfolios on Learning*, British Educational Communications and Technology Agency, Coventry.

—— (2007b) *Learning Platforms and Personalised Learning*, British Educational Communications and Technology Agency, Coventry.

—— (2007c) *Harnessing Technology Review 2007: Progress and Impact of Technology in Education*, British Educational Communications and Technology Agency, Coventry.

—— (2007d) *October Board – Paper 2 – Update on the Home Access Taskforce*, British Educational Communications and Technology Agency, Coventry.

Boyle, H. (2006) *Opening Minds: A Competency-based Curriculum for the Twenty-first Century*, National Teacher Research Panel.

Bradbrook, G., Alvi, I., Fisher, J., Lloyd, H., Brake, D., Helsper, E. and Livingstone, S. (2008) *Meeting their Potential: The Role of Education and Technology in Overcoming Disadvantage and Disaffection in Young People*, British Educational Communications and Technology Agency, Coventry.

Brandon, M., Howe, A., Dagley, V., Salter, C., Warren, C. and Black, J. (2006) *Evaluating the Common Assessment Framework and Lead Professional Guidance and Implementation 2005–6*, Department for Education and Skills, London.

Buckley, D. (2007) *The Personalisation by Pieces Framework*, Cambridge Education Associates, Cambridge.

CfP (2006) 'Computers for Pupils, Guidance for LAs and Schools, 2006–08', Computers for Pupils (now at Becta, Coventry, www.teachernet.gov.uk/wholeschool/ictis/computers_for_pupils).

Coffield, F., Moseley, D., Hall, E. and Ecclestone, K. (2004) *Learning Styles and Pedagogy in post-16 Learning*, British Educational Communications and Technology Agency, Coventry, www.lsda.org.uk/files/PDF/1543.pdf

Condie, R., Munro, B., Seagraves, L. and Kenesson, S. (2007) *The Impact of ICT in Schools – A Landscape Review*, British Educational Communications and Technology Agency, Coventry.

Daanen, H. and Facer, K. (2007) *2020 and Beyond*, Futurelab, Bristol.

DCSF (2007a) *Publication of 2007 Test and Examination Results in the School and College Achievement and Attainment Tables*, Department for Children, Schools and Families, London.

—— (2007b) 'ContactPoint: Q and A', Department for Children, Schools and Families, London, www.everychildmatters.gov.uk/deliveringservices/contactpoint

—— (2008a) *An Introduction to Building Schools for the Future*, Department for Children, Schools and Families, London.

—— (2008b) *ContactPoint Data Security Review*, Department for Children, Schools and Families, London.

—— (2008c) *Safer Children in a Digital World: The Report of the Byron Review*, Department for Children, Schools and Families, London, www.dfes.gov.uk/byronreview

DfES (2001) *Special Educational Needs Code of Practice*, Department for Education and Skills, London.

—— (2002) *Transforming the Way we Learn: A Vision for the Future of ICT in Schools*, Department for Education and Skills, London.

—— (2004a) *Every Child Matters: Change for Children*, Department for Education and Skills, London.

—— (2004b) *The School Library and the Key Stage 3 National Strategy*, Department for Education and Skills, London.

—— (2004c) *Removing Barriers to Achievement*, Department for Education and Skills, London.

—— (2005a) *Harnessing Technology: Transforming Learning and Children's Services*, Department for Education and Skills, London.

—— (2005b) *Extended Schools, Access to Services and Opportunities for All*, Department for Education and Skills, London.

—— (2006) *2020 Vision: Report of the Teaching and Learning in 2020 Review Group*, Department for Education and Skills, London.

—— (2007a) *Extended Schools: Building on Experience*, Department for Education and Skills, London.

—— (2007b) *Pedagogy and Personalisation, Primary and Secondary National Strategies*, Department for Education and Skills, London.

EC (2008) *Working Document 1/2008 on the protection of children's personal data (General guidelines and the special case of schools)*, Article 29 Data Protection Working Party, European Commission, Brussels.

Education Queensland (undated) 'The New Basics Project', Department of Education, Training and the Arts, Queensland, Australia, http://education.qld.gov.au/corporate/newbasics

Education Queensland (2001) 'The Rich Tasks', Department of Education, Training and the Arts, Queensland, Australia, http://education.qld.gov.au/corporate/newbasics/html/richtasks/richtasks.html

ELSPA (2006) Unlimited Learning, Computer and video games in the learning landscape, Entertainment & Leisure Software Publishers Association, London.

Fielding, M. (2006) 'Leadership, personalization and high performance schooling: naming the new totalitarianism', *School Leadership & Management* 26: 347–69.

Fuchs, T. and Woessmann, L. (2004) *Computers and Student Learning: Bivariate and Multivariate Evidence on the Availability and Use of Computers at Home and at School*, University of Munich.

Futurelab (2008) 'Can every child matter? (and if so, how?)', *Vision* (6): 9–12.

Gardner, H. (2000) 'Can technology exploit our many ways of knowing?', in D.T. Gordon (ed.), *The Digital Classroom: How Technology is Changing the Way We Teach and Learn*, Harvard Education, Cambridge, MA, USA, pp. 32–35.

Gardner, H. and Veenema, S. (1996) Multimedia and multiple intelligences, *The American Prospect*, 7 (29): 69–75.

Grant, L. (2007) *Learning to be Part of the Knowledge Economy: Digital Divides and Media Literacy*, Futurelab, Bristol.

Green, H. and Hannon, C. (2007) *Their Space: Education for a Digital Generation*, Demos, London.

Green, H., Facer, K. and Rudd, T. (2005) *Personalisation and Digital Technologies*, Futurelab, Bristol.

Harbird, R. (2006) *Novel Applications for Information Technology in Risk Assessment for Children's Social Care in the UK*, Research Note RN/06/11, University College London.

Hargreaves, D. (2003) *Education Epidemic: Transforming Secondary Schools through Innovation Networks*, Demos, London.

HM Government (2004) *The Children Act*, available at www.opsi.gov.uk

HM Treasury/DCSF (2007) *Aiming High for Young People: A Ten Year Strategy for Positive Activities*, HM Treasury, London.

Jackson, D., Cordingley, P. and Hannon, V. (2004) *Networked Learning Communities: Programme, Policy Environment and the Potential of Participatory Evaluation*, National College for School Leadership, Nottingham.

Johnson, M. (2004) *Personalised Learning – An Emperor's Outfit?* Demos, London.

Kendall, L., O'Donnell, L., Golden, S., Ridley, K., Machin, S., Rutt, S., McNally, S., Schagen, I., Meghir, C., Stoney, S., Morris, M., West, A. and Noden, P. (2005)

Excellence in Cities: The National Evaluation of a Policy to Raise Standards in Urban Schools 2000–2003, National Foundation for Educational Research, Slough.

Leadbetter, C. (2004) *Learning about Personalisation: How Can We Put the Learner at the Heart of the Education System?*, Department for Education and Skills, London.

—— (2005) *The Shape of Things to Come: Personalised Learning through Collaboration*, Department for Education and Skills, London.

—— (2007) *Social Software for Social Change*, Office of the Third Sector, Cabinet Office, London.

Leadbetter, C., Bartlett, J. and Gallagher, N. (2008) *Making it Personal*, Demos, London.

Leitch, S. (2006) *Prosperity for All in the Global Economy – World Class Skills*, Stationery Office, Norwich, www.hm-treasury.gov.uk/independent_reviews/leitch_rev iew/review_leitch_index.cfm

Livingstone, S. and Bober, M. (2004) 'Taking up online opportunities? Children's uses of the internet for education, communication and participation' *E-Learning* 1(3): 395–419, www.wwwords.co.uk/elea

—— (2005) *UK Children Go Online: Final Report of Key Project Findings*, Economic and Social Research Council, London.

Livingstone, S. and Bovill, M. (1999) *Young People: New Media*, London School of Economics and Political Science.

Machin, S., McNally, S. and Silva, O. (2006) *New Technology in Schools: Is There a Payoff?*, Discussion Paper No. 2234, Institute for the Study of Labor (IZA), Bonn, http://ftp.iza.org/dp2234.pdf

—— (2007) 'Educational Benefits from Computers in Schools', Media Briefing, July, Royal Economics Society, University of St Andrews, Scotland.

Madden, A.D., Baptista Nunes, J.M., McPherson, M., Ford, N.J. and Miller, D. (2005) *A New Generation Gap? Some Thoughts on the Consequences of Increasingly Early ICT First Contact*, White Rose University Consortium (Universities of York, Leeds and Sheffield).

Marks, K. (2006) *Mobile Traveller Children: Steps in Bridging the Digital Divide: A Summary of the Full Evaluation Report of the E-LAMP3 Project*, National Association of Teachers of Travellers, University of Sheffield.

McFarlane, A. (1999) *ILS, A Guide to Good Practice*, British Educational Communications and Technology Agency, Coventry.

Melis, E. and Monthienvichienchai, R (2004) *They Call it Learning Style But it's So Much More*, London Knowledge Lab, Institute of Education.

Miliband, D. (2004) 'Choice and voice in personalised learning', speech delivered at DfES Innovation Unit/Demos/OECD Conference, 'Personalising Education: The Future of Public Sector Reform', London, 18 May 2004, www.dfes.gov.uk/speeches/media/documents/PLfinal.doc

Morgan, J., Williamson, B., Lee, T. and Facer, K. (2007) *Enquiring Minds: A Guide*, Futurelab, Bristol.

Morgan, R. (2007) *Making ContactPoint Work: Children's Views on the Government Guidance*, A report by the Children's Rights Director for England, Ofsted, Manchester.

Mulhern, P. (2003) Competing Values, Policy Ambiguity: A Study of Mainstream Primary Teachers' Views of 'Inclusive Education', *Educate – The Journal of Doctoral Research in Education* 3(1): 5–10.

Neethling, K. (2000) 'Getting to Grips with Your Whole Brain', DVD, Neethling Brain Instruments, Johannesburg, www.solutionsfinding.com

Norwich, B. (2008) *Dilemmas of Difference, Inclusion and Disability: International Perspectives and Future Directions*, Routledge, London.

ODPM (2005) *Inclusion through Innovation: Tackling Social Exclusion through New Technologies*, Office of the Deputy Prime Minister, London.

Ofsted (2005a) *A New Relationship with Schools: Improving Performance through School Self-Evaluation*, Ofsted, Manchester.

—— (2005b) *Embedding ICT in Schools – A Dual Evaluation Exercise*, Ofsted, Manchester.

—— (2006a) *Extended Services in Schools and Children's Centres*, Ofsted, Manchester.

—— (2006b) *Inclusion: Does it Matter where Children are Taught?*, Ofsted, Manchester.

—— (2007) *Assessing the Impact of ICT in Schools*, Ofsted, Manchester.

ONS (1998) *Survey of Information and Communications Technology in Schools*, Office for National Statistics, London.

Owen, M. (2004) *An Anatomy of Games*, Futurelab, Bristol.

Owen, M., Grant, L., Sayers, S. and Facer, K. (2006) *Social Software and Learning*, Futurelab, Bristol.

Page, B. (2007) 'Understanding Learners', presentation to Becta 'Harnessing Technology: Building on Success' National Conference, Ipsos Mori Social Research Institute, London.

Parker, S., Tims, C. and Wright, S. (2006) *Inclusion, Innovation and Democracy: Growing Talent for the Creative and Cultural Industries*, Demos, London.

Prensky, M. (2001) 'Digital Natives, Digital Immigrants, Part Two: Do They Really Think Differently?', *On the Horizon* (NCB University Press) 9(6).

Prior, G. and Hall, L. (2003) *ICT in Schools Survey 2004*, Department for Education and Skills, London. Available at www.becta.org.uk/research (select Archive).

QCA (1999) *The National Curriculum*, Qualifications and Curriculum Authority, London.

Rachlin, H. (undated) 'Burrhus Frederic Skinner: March 20, 1904–August 18, 1990', Biographical Memoir, National Academy of Sciences, Washington, DC, USA, www.nap.edu/readingroom/books/biomems/bskinner.html

RSA (2002) *Opening Minds Project Update*, Royal Society for the Arts, London.

Royle, K. and Clarke, C. (2003) 'Making the Case For Computer Games as a Learning Environment', position paper, University of Wolverhampton, www.desq.co.uk/doomed/pdf/Making_the_case.pdf

Rudd, T., Colligan, F. and Naik, R. (2006) *Learner Voice*, Futurelab, Bristol.

Sandford, R. and Williamson, B. (2005) *Games and Learning*, Futurelab, Bristol.

Sandford, R., Ulicsak, M., Facer, K. and Rudd, T. (2006) *Teaching with Games: Using Commercial Off-the-shelf Computer Games in Formal Education*, Futurelab, Bristol.

Schmitt, J. and Wadsworth, J. (2004) *Is There an Impact of Household Computer Ownership on Children's Educational Attainment in Britain?* Centre for Economic Performance, London School of Economics.

Selwyn, N. and Young, M (2007) 'Rethinking Schools, Knowledge and Technology', seminar paper delivered at London Knowledge Lab, May 2007, the Institute of Education and Birkbeck College, London, www.lkl.ac.uk

Smith, A., Lovatt, M. and Wise, D. (2003) *Accelerated Learning, A User's Guide*, Network Educational Press, Stafford.

Sparrowhawk, A. (2007) *Digital Resources to Support Basic Skills Education for 14–19 year olds*, Futurelab, Bristol.

Underwood, J., Baguley, T., Banyard, P., Coyne, E., Farrington-Flint, L. and Selwood, I. (2007) *Impact 2007: Personalising Learning with Technology*, British Educational Communications and Technology Agency, Coventry.

Ward, H. (2006) 'Goodbye Computer Chips', *Times Educational Supplement*, 19 May.

Williamson, B. (2003) *Bridging or Broadening the Digital Divide: Interfacing the Experience of Learning for the Next Decade*, Futurelab, Bristol.

Index